MW00936243

Ramana Maharshi:

His Life

by
Gabriele Ebert

Foreword
by
Alan Adams-Jacobs

Translated
by
Victor Ward

Gabriele Ebert
Ramana Maharshi: His Life
translated from German into English by Victor Ward
Norderstedt: Books on Demand
3rd edition, 2015
ISBN 978-3-7392-1039-1

title of the original edition: Ramana Maharshi: Sein Leben. – Lüchow Verlag : Stuttgart, 2003

Book cover: BoD
Photos with permission from Sri Ramanasramam
Printed in Germany

Sri Ramana Maharshi

Table of Contents

Foreword
by Alan Adams-Jacobs

Ramana Maharshi is universally considered as the Greatest Sage that has been born, as an act of Divine grace, on this planet for a millennium. Not since Adi *Shankara* has any Enlightened Being made such an impact on the spiritual development of our world both in the East and in the West.

This beautifully written and most expertly translated major biography of the Great Master fully illustrates this claim, most convincingly and in no uncertain manner. It is full of anecdotal history which brings to vivid life, the teachings and example of this supreme Spiritual Master.

He lived an exemplary life, beyond any fault and blemish. He was an example of moral purity and intellectual clarity. He was an inspiring Poet and wise Philosopher, but above all he largely taught through Silence. This is the rarest gift, even amongst Great Sages, and is the hallmark of the highest, most evolved example of humanity. In his personal life he was a model of love and compassion embracing all who came to him with true equanimity, and never refused guidance to any who approached him.

He was revolutionary and radical because he made his simple unique Direct Path to Self Realization available to all men and women who were earnest in their quest. The only qualification was a strong desire for liberation from the bondage of suffering in an illusory world. His simple method of Self Enquiry and Self Surrender did away with all the complicated and confusing spiritual practices and bizarre theories which have blurred and muddled the Path to Enlightenment for thousands of years. His way is available to every householder. It is an open secret. The only qualification is sincerity, and a serious intent to make effort along the lines he suggested.

He came to the Planet prepared to bring his message at one of the darkest times for our humanity when a great light was needed to restore the *Dharma* of Truth and Righteousness. His *Maha-yoga* embraces all the traditional paths of Devotion, Work, and Knowledge. It is available, without any change in life style for the ordinary householder. There is no longer any need to follow a monastic way to live a truly religious life in the twenty-first century.

As this book and many others, amply illustrate, he brought many of his devotees to Self Realization. His influence and guidance is still experienced today, even after his death, by those who are conscientiously practising his teaching. Most importantly he is responsible for the Renaissance of the *Advaita* Movement which is sweeping West and East like wildfire in the dense forest of *samsara*, and bringing much needed spiritual help to many thousands.

This book skilfully and meticulously written by Gabriele Ebert, with famed Teutonic thoroughness, devotedly recounts his life story in a masterly and scholarly manner. She is a child of our contemporary Western culture, so her book can be readily enjoyed by the Western, as well as by the Eastern reader. It was no less a personage than C.G. Jung who wrote in his essay on the Maharshi that in India he is the whitest spot in a white space. Could there be a higher commendation?

It is a privilege to heartily recommend this beautiful book to all those who are earnest in their spiritual quest and who genuinely wish to learn more about this Great Sage, his life and his teachings. I am confident it will thrill and instruct all those who are open to the possibility of Self Realization, now, for themselves, in this God-given life. It is a second education for those who see that all their life hitherto has been merely a preparation.

Alan Adams-Jacobs
Chairman, Ramana Maharshi Foundation UK
October 2003, Hampstead, London

Introduction

Sri Ramana Maharshi, who has opened up the path of *advaita* to all people, is one of the most remarkable Sages of the modern era. After his enlightenment at age 17 he led a simple life on the sacred Hill Arunachala, in Southern India, for over 50 years, until his death in 1950. Attracted by the power of his presence, people from all countries, cultures and religions, whether rich or poor, educated or uneducated, came in their thousands to see him. Since his death nothing has changed, on the contrary, Ramanashram and Arunachala have become a vibrant spiritual centre and more and more people are showing an interest in the teachings of Ramana Maharshi.

There was a great deal of source material available for this new biography, as, over the last 50 years, many of the Maharshi's devotees have published their recollections and diaries. The bibliography contains a list of all the sources used. The quotes included at the beginning of each chapter are direct quotes from Sri Ramana himself, unless otherwise indicated. Sanskrit terms are printed in italics and are explained in the glossary. Photos showing places today have been taken by me.

Acknowledgements

I would like to thank Victor Ward for this excellent translation, Alan Adams-Jacobs for the wonderful foreword and Miles Wright for his help in compiling the glossary and for looking through Chapter 18. Robert Högerle's helpful suggestions were also very much appreciated. I am also extremely grateful to the President of Ramanashram - Sri V.S. Ramanan, and the President of the Ramana Maharshi Foundation in Bangalore - Sri A.R. Natarajan, for their authorisation to use the Indian publications and photo material.

1. Birth and Childhood

What value has this birth without knowledge born of realization?

Ramana's home at Tiruchuli

Venkataraman, later to be known as Ramana Maharshi, was born into an old Brahmin family on 30th December 1879 in Tiruchuli, a village of approximately 500 houses some 30 miles south of Madurai in Tamil Nadu, South India. Tiruchuli is the administrative centre (Taluk) for the Ramnad District. There has been a village on this spot for many centuries and it is mentioned in several legends in the *Puranas*. The Bhuminatheswara temple, dedicated to *Shiva* as Lord of the World, is a very popular place of pilgrimage. People often bathe in the temple tank, as it is claimed that the high sulphur content of the water has healing properties.

Sri Ramana's father, Sundaram Iyer, started his professional life at the age of twelve as a clerk for a village accountant. He later became a petition writer and ultimately worked his way up to the post of uncertified pleader (Vakil). He practised principally at the local court of arbitration and earned sufficient money to enable him to provide a comfortable life for his family. He was considered to be both extremely skilled and fair and had a reputation for dealing kindly with the poor and oppressed. He was highly respected in the local courts, so much so that on occasions both parties, plaintiff and defendant, wanted him to plead on their behalf.

Ramana's father Sundaram

Sundaram was also well-known for his great generosity and hospitality. His spacious house in Kartikeyan Street near the temple had two separate areas with identical furnishings and fittings. One area was used by the family, the other was made available to guests. Any poor person who knocked at the door was provided with a meal. Countless clients and visitors came to the house throughout the day. Sundaram also offered accommodation and assistance to any newly arrived officials, until they found permanent lodgings of their own.

In so far as concerns spiritual matters Sundaram was very ordinary. His spiritual life, like that of every other devout Hindu, involved occasional pilgrimages to local temples, reading the legends of Hindu Saints and performance of the daily domestic puja.

Sri Ramana's mother, Alagammal, came from Pasalai, a village near Manamadurai. She was married to Sundaram Iyer when she was still a child. There was no formal school education for women at that time, but from the elder women in Tiruchuli she learned many *vedantic* hymns, from which she took the spiritual instruction for her life.

She and her husband were an ideal couple. She supported Sundaram's hospitality in every way, even if it meant she had to prepare a meal for guests in the middle of the night. The harmony between them was further emphasized through their names - Sundaram means 'beauty' in Sanskrit, while Alagammal means 'beauty' in Tamil. Ramana wrote in one of his hymns to Arunachala, "May Thou and I be one and inseparable like Alagu and Sundaram, Oh Arunachala."

Ramana was born one hour after midnight on Monday, 30th December 1879, as the second of three sons and one daughter. Throughout Southern India it was the day of the *Arudra Darshan*, the festival of the cosmic dance of *Shiva Nataraja*. That year this special festival day lasted from sunrise on the 29th to sunrise on the 30th December. At dawn on the 29th the devotees of *Shiva* took their ritual bath in the temple tank. Afterwards the flower-bedecked statue of *Nataraja* was carried through the streets of the village to the sound of drums and bells and much singing. At 1 a.m. it was returned to the temple of Tiruchuli where the customary rituals were performed. Venkataraman was born at that precise moment. It is recorded that a blind woman present in the delivery room had a vision of a wondrous light and said, "He who is born today in your house must be a divine being."

Sundaram named his second oldest son Venkataraman. Ramana is an abbreviation of Venkataraman, but nobody, with the exception of one relative, ever called him that. Later Ganapati Muni (see Chapter 8) used the name 'Ramana Maharshi' and it is only since this time that 'Ramana' has been in use.

Venkataraman's childhood was completely normal. He was a strong boy and was breast-fed by his mother until he was five years old. He was friendly and open-minded by nature and was loved by everyone in the village. He attended the local primary school in Tiruchuli for three years before going to the secondary school in Dindigul when he was eleven. Whereas his elder brother, Nagaswami, was a diligent pupil, Venkataraman, although intelligent, took little delight in learning. He was far more interested in sports and games. The Bhuminatheswara temple and its surroundings were his favourite playground. He liked to meet with his friends there at the temple tank. A phenomenon which remains unexplained even today, is the change in water level in the Tamil month of Masi (mid-February to mid-March), with the waxing moon the water rises approximately 12 inches a day for ten days in a row, then subsides with the waning moon back to its original level. Ramana remembered how, fascinated, he used to watch this as a boy, "In my boyhood days, all of us used to join together and draw on the steps some signs in order to see how much the water rose each day. It used to be amusing. The rising of the water used to start 10 days earlier [before the full moon] and used to submerge the steps at the rate of one step per day and become full by the full moon day. To us, it was great fun."[1]

Another of Ramana's playgrounds was the Gaundinya river near the Kalayar temple on the outskirts of Tiruchuli. There he and his friends used to swim or play together inside the temple area.

Not a great deal is known about this period of Ramana's life, but what is known makes it clear that he was a lively boy who liked to play pranks.

One day, when he was about six years old, he climbed up to the loft of his house along with some friends. The place was full of bundles of old papers and documents, which his father had decided to store there and which related to lawsuits long-since settled. The children took one of the bundles down and made a fleet of paper boats out of it, which they then sailed in the temple tank. When Ramana's father came home, he was furious, so Ramana quickly made himself scarce. When he did not return for the midday meal, a search was organized. He was found sitting in the temple in the shrine of

---

[1] Nagamma: Letters and Recollections, p. 78

goddess Sahayambal (one of *Shiva's* consorts), from whom he had sought solace.

On another occasion Ramana went even further, he climbed into the house of a neighbouring lawyer and carried away some papers he found in a cupboard, unaware that they were important documents relating to a court case. He invented a game for himself, distributing the documents to passers-by on the street, as if they were advertising leaflets. When the lawyer returned home and saw what had happened, he demanded the papers back, but it proved impossible to recover many of them. Of course when he told Ramana's father what had happened, the latter became very angry and shouted, "Undress the boy! Shave his head completely and give him only a loincloth to wear! Don't give him any food!" How far the punishment was carried out is, unfortunately, not reported.

Ramana, however, in addition to his predilection for playing pranks, also had a compassionate heart, as is illustrated by the following story, which he later recounted himself, "One day he [referring to a neighbouring boy three years his younger] got a sugarcane and a knife, and as he could not cut it himself, he requested his brothers to help him, but they went away without heeding his request. He began weeping. I felt sorry for him. I took the sugarcane and tried to cut it. My finger got cut and began to bleed. Even so, I felt sorry for him because he was weeping and was a little fellow, so somehow I managed to cut the cane into pieces. I tied my finger with a wet cloth; the bleeding, however did not stop."[2]

The rite of Upanayama (putting on the sacred Brahmin thread) was performed when Ramana was around the age of eight, and he thus became a full member of the Brahmin caste, but still he showed no special spiritual inclination.

Although this fortunate family was no more religious than any other, there was one peculiar feature in its history. An old family legend

---

[2] dto., p. 80

tells how, one day, an ascetic came to the house begging for food, but, against all tradition, he was not treated with the proper respect and was not given a meal. The ascetic promptly issued a curse, stating that henceforth one member of each generation of the family would wander about begging as an ascetic like himself. This 'curse' had its effect, because in each generation one member renounced worldly life to become a wandering ascetic. One of Sundaram Iyer's uncles on his father's side had taken the ochre robe, the staff and the water jug of a *sannyasin* and had left to live life as a wandering renunciant and beggar. His elder brother Venkatesa also disappeared from the village one day, no doubt to embark upon the same path. He was never heard of again and since that time Sundaram had been the head of the family.

There are no indications that Sundaram Iyer ever thought that one of his sons would one day also leave home. And no doubt the thought never crossed the mind of the young Ramana either.

2. The Awakening to the True Self

All this was not a mere intellectual process, but flashed before me vividly as living truth, something which I perceived immediately, without any argument almost. 'I' was something very real, the only real thing in that state.

In Madurai

Ramana's home at Madurai

In February 1892 Sundaram Iyer unexpectedly died, he was in his mid-forties. He left behind him his wife Alagammal, their three sons, Nagaswami aged fourteen, Ramana aged twelve and Nagasundaram aged six and their daughter Alamelu aged four. When Ramana returned from his school at Dindigul to Tiruchuli, to see his dead father for the last time, he reflected thoughtfully, "When Father is lying here, why do they say that he has gone?" One of the elders answered him, "If this were your father, would he not receive you with love? So you see, he has gone."

The sudden death of the head of the family was a dramatic event which resulted in the family being split up. Alagammal moved to Manamadurai with the younger children Nagasundaram and Alamelu to live with her younger brother-in-law Nelliappa Iyer, who was also working as a pleader. The two older children moved into the house of Subba Iyer, another uncle on the father's side, who lived at number 11 Chokkappa Naicken Street near the famous *Meenakshi* temple.

Ramana was sent to Scott's Middle School and later to the American Mission High School. He was an average scholar who learned easily, but was not much interested in his lessons. He would often go unprepared to class. If others recited the day's lesson he would remember enough to enable him to keep up.

Later he told his devotees the following story with regard to his schooldays, "While the school lessons were being taught, lest I should fall asleep I used to tie a thread to the nail on the wall, and tie my hair to it. When the head nods, the thread is pulled tight and that used to wake me up. Otherwise, the teacher used to twist my ears and wake me up."[3]

Wrestling, boxing, running and other sports were much more appealing to Ramana. He was stronger than most boys of his age and his strength and ability even impressed the older boys. He also liked to play football with his friends. People noticed that his team always won. This and other similar occurrences earned him the nickname 'Thangakai' (Golden Hand). It is a title given in Tamil Nadu to people who are always successful in their undertakings.

In his uncle's house there was a room on the upper floor that was largely unused. Here Ramana used to play 'throw-ball' with his friends, with the young Ramana himself as the 'ball'. He would curl

---

[3] Nagamma: Letters, p. 175

himself up into a ball and the other playmates would throw him from one to another. Sometimes they failed to catch him and he landed on the floor, but he was never hurt by this rough play. This room in which he played is the same room in which he later had his death experience.

Sometimes Ramana and his brother would sneak out of the house at night to roam about with their playmates near the Vaigai river or the Pillaiyarpaliam tank in the outskirts of Madurai. "Every night, when the whole house was silent in sleep, Nagaswami and Ramana whose beds were in a remote corner of the house, would appropriately adjust their pillows and cover them up with their bed sheets so that it would create the impression of their presence in their beds. It was the duty of little Venkataraman [a younger friend of the same name] to bolt the door of the house when the brothers went out at about 11 p.m., and to admit them on their return at about 4 a.m."[4]

Ramana did not study Sanskrit or the sacred traditions of Hinduism such as the *Vedas* or the *Upanishads*. In both the schools he attended he was taught Christianity, but Hindu boys generally showed little interest in such bible classes – and Ramana was no exception in this respect.

Although he was very much like any other boy, he did have one peculiar trait. His sleep used to be exceptionally deep. When a relative later visited him at the Ashram Ramana recalled the following incident which happened in Dindigul, "Your uncle Periappa Seshaiyar was living there then. There was some function in the house and all went to it and then in the night went to the temple. I was left alone in the house. I was sitting reading in the front room, but after a while I locked the front door and fastened the windows and went to sleep. When they returned from the temple no amount of shouting or banging at the door or window could wake me. At last they managed to open the door with a key from the opposite house and then they tried to wake me up by beating me. All

---

[4] Krishnamurti Aiyer: Sri Ramana's Boyhood in Madurai. In: Ramana Smrti, p. [58]

the boys beat me to their heart's content, and your uncle did too, but without effect. I knew nothing about it till they told me next morning. ... The same sort of thing happened to me in Madurai too. The boys didn't dare to touch me when I was awake, but if they had any grudge against me they would come when I was asleep and carry me wherever they liked and beat me as much as they liked and then put me back to bed, and I would know nothing about it until they told me in the morning."[5]

The Death Experience

Arunachala

The event that heralded Ramana's spiritual awakening was an incident in November 1895, shortly before his sixteenth birthday, according to the western calculation, his seventeenth birthday according to Indian calculation. For the first time he heard mentioned the holy mountain Arunachala, the place to which he would soon set off and where he was to live until his death.

---

[5] Mudaliar: Day by Day, p. 209

Arunachala (transl.: the Red Mountain) on the wide plain of Southern India is geologically one of the oldest parts of the earth. For pious Hindus it is one of the most sacred pilgrimage sites. There is a well-known saying in Southern India which the young Ramana also knew, "To see Chidambaram, to be born at Tiruvarur, to die at Benares or even to think of Arunachala is to be assured of Liberation."[6]

At the time Ramana only knew that Arunachala was a very holy place. He had never connected it with any real place and did not know where the mountain was located. Nevertheless, from childhood onwards, he had been aware of a kind of permanent pulsating repetition (sphurana) of "Arunachala, Arunachala", that was both spontaneous and uninterrupted.

One day in November 1895 he met an elderly relative and when he asked him where he was coming from, the answer came back, "from Arunachala". For the first time Ramana learned that Arunachala was a real place which one could visit. He further asked where it was situated and received the answer, "What! Do you not know Tiruvannamalai? That is Arunachalam." Of course the town of Tiruvannamalai was well known to him.

Soon thereafter, in the middle of July 1896, at the age of 16, the great change took place in his life. He was at the time a pupil in his final year at secondary school. He later described the incident which changed his life completely and irreversibly, "It was about six weeks before I left Madurai for good that the great change in my life took place. It was so sudden. One day I sat up alone on the first floor of my uncle's house. I was in my usual health. I seldom had any illness. I was a heavy sleeper. ... So, on that day as I sat alone there was nothing wrong with my health. But a sudden and unmistakable

---

[6]According to the Sthalapuranam. In the inmost sanctuary of the temple at Chidambaram is the Golden Hall with the main sculpture of *Shiva Natarajan*. Tiruvarur belongs to the largest temple complexes in Southern India. Benares (Varanasi) on the holy Ganges is the town of *Shiva* and the most holy of all places of Hindu pilgrimage.

fear of death seized me. I felt I was going to die. Why I should have so felt cannot now be explained by anything felt in my body. Nor could I explain it to myself then. I did not however trouble myself to discover if the fear was well grounded. I felt 'I was going to die,' and at once set about thinking out what I should do. I did not care to consult doctors or elders or even friends. I felt I had to solve the problem myself then and there.

The shock of fear of death made me at once introspective, or 'introverted'. I said to myself mentally, i.e., without uttering the words – 'Now, death has come. What does it mean? What is it that is dying? This body dies.' I at once dramatized the scene of death. I extended my limbs and held them rigid as though rigor-mortis had set in. I imitated a corpse to lend an air of reality to my further investigation. I held my breath and kept my mouth closed, pressing the lips tightly together so that no sound might escape. Let not the word 'I' or any other word be uttered! 'Well then,' said I to myself, 'this body is dead. It will be carried stiff to the burning ground and there burnt and reduced to ashes. But with the death of this body, am "I" dead? Is the body "I"? This body is silent and inert. But I feel the full force of my personality and even the sound "I" within myself, - apart from the body. So "I" am a spirit, a thing transcending the body. The material body dies, but the spirit transcending it cannot be touched by death. I am therefore the deathless spirit.'

All this was not a mere intellectual process, but flashed before me vividly as living truth, something which I perceived immediately, without any argument almost. 'I' was something very real, the only real thing in that state, and all the conscious activity that was connected with my body was centred on that. The 'I' or my 'self' was holding the focus of attention by a powerful fascination from that time forwards. Fear of death had vanished once and forever. Absorption in the Self has continued from that moment right up to this time. Other thoughts may come and go like the various notes of a musician, but the 'I' continues like the basic or fundamental sruti note which accompanies and blends with all other notes. Whether the body was engaged in talking, reading or anything else, I was still centred on 'I'.

Previous to that crisis I had no clear perception of myself and was not consciously attracted to it. I had felt no direct perceptible interest in it, much less any permanent disposition to dwell upon it."[7]

Later it was said on more than one occasion that Ramana's experience had lasted approximately 20 minutes or half an hour. But he himself stressed that there was no concept of time in it.

It is also remarkable that afterwards Ramana never harboured any doubts concerning his Self Realization. The experience remained with him thereafter uninterrupted and was never lost or diminished. He had absolutely no doubts about it and never searched confirmation from a spiritual teacher. He repeatedly stressed in later years, that despite the apparent changing phases of his outward life there was never any change in this experience and he always remained the same.

As a result of this death experience Ramana's life was instantly and totally changed. He reports, "When I lay down with limbs outstretched and mentally enacted the death scene and realized that the body would be taken and cremated and yet I would live, some force, call it atmic power [power of *atman*] or anything else, rose within me and took possession of me. With that, I was reborn and I became a new man. I became indifferent to everything afterwards, having neither likes nor dislikes."[8]

From now on he swallowed everything that was served to him, whether delicious or tasteless, good or bad, with no regard to how it tasted or smelled, or to its quality. Formerly, if he thought an injustice had been done to him or if other boys teased him, he would stand up for himself. Now he accepted everything without protest. He was also no longer interested in joining in his friends' sporting

---

[7] Narasimha Swami: Self Realization, pp. 20-22
[8] Mudaliar: Day by Day, p. 41

activities, but rather sat alone and meditated with eyes closed in yogic posture. At school he started to encounter problems, because he was no longer interested in books. He remembered, "After the 'death' experience I was living in a different world. How could I turn my attention to books? Before that, I would at least attend to what the other boys repeated and repeat the same myself. But afterwards, I could not do even that. At school, my mind would not dwell on study at all. I would be imagining and expecting God would suddenly drop down from Heaven before me."[9]

Though Ramana told nobody about his great experience and tried to appear as before, other people of course noticed the change which had come over him. His elder brother Nagaswami made fun of him and called him a *jnani* (enlightened being) or yogiswara (highest of all yogis) and said mockingly that he would do better to take himself off to some dense primeval forest like the seers (*rishis*) of old.

Devotion to God (Bhakti)

After the death experience, *bhakti*, the loving veneration of and devotion to God, gained in importance for Ramana. Some months before his enlightenment he had read the first spiritual book in his life, Sekkilar's *Periyapuranam*, the life story of the 63 Tamil saints (nayanars). Their statues can be found in the *Meenakshi* temple in Madurai. Ancient legends tell how the 63 saints had obtained *Shiva's* grace and had renounced everything and left home.

After his enlightenment Ramana started to visit the temple regularly. He recalled, "Formerly I would go there rarely with friends, see the images, put on sacred ashes and sacred vermilion on the forehead and return home without any perceptible emotion. After the awakening into the new life, I would go almost every evening to the temple. I would go alone and stand before *Shiva*, or *Meenakshi* or *Nataraja* or the sixty-three saints for long periods. I would feel

---

[9] dto., p. 279

waves of emotion overcoming me. The former hold on the body had been given up by my spirit, since it ceased to cherish the idea I-am-the-body. The spirit therefore longed to have a fresh hold and hence the frequent visits to the temple and the overflow of the soul in profuse tears. This was God's (*Isvara's*) play with the individual spirit. I would stand before *Isvara*, the Controller of the universe and the destinies of all, the Omniscient and Omnipresent, and occasionally pray for the descent of his grace upon me so that my devotion might increase and become perpetual like that of the sixty-three saints. Mostly I would not pray at all, but let the deep within flow on and into the deep without. Tears would mark this overflow of the soul and not betoken any particular feeling of pleasure or pain."[10]

During his last month in Madurai, Ramana suffered from an unusual intense pain in his head and a burning sensation. But all symptoms of his profound change disappeared when he stepped into the temple at Tiruvannamalai for the first time on 1st September 1896.

---

[10] Narasimha Swami: Self Realization, pp. 23ff

3. Departure for Arunachala

When I left home, I was like a speck swept on by a tremendous flood,
I knew not my body or the world, whether it was day or night.

Ramana's farewell letter

Ramana now faced a continual conflict between the demands placed upon him by his everyday life in the form of family and teachers, and absorption in the Self, which was now almost constant. This conflict could not last for ever and on 29th August 1896, approximately six weeks after his enlightenment, it finally came to a head. One day he had failed to study properly some lesson on English grammar. As punishment for this he had been given the task of copying out the lesson three times. When he came to the third copy his mind revolted against this soulless mechanical exercise. He pushed the work aside, sat upright in yoga posture, closed his eyes and started to meditate. His elder brother Nagaswami, who had been watching him all the time, cried out ill-temperedly, "Why should one, who behaves thus, retain all this?" The meaning was, that for one who behaves like a *sadhu*, family life and school made no sense anymore and he had no right to the comforts of domestic life. It was not the first time his brother had made such remarks and reproaches. But this time the shot went home.

Ramana saw that what his brother said was true. At the same moment the thought of Arunachala took full possession of him. He understood that the strong attraction which he felt was a call and decided there and then to set off for Arunachala. He knew, however, that his family would not let him go if he were to explain his plans to them, so he devised a scheme which would enable him to leave secretly. He told his brother that he had to attend a special class in electricity at school at 12 noon. Nagaswami, who had no idea of what was going on in his younger brother's mind, said, "Well then, do not fail to take five rupees from the box below, and to pay my college fees."

Ramana went downstairs, ate quickly and obtained the five rupees from his uncle's wife. He, of course, told her nothing about his plan. He later reflected that this white lie, which was the only one he told during his life, was necessary to enable him to come to Tiruvannamalai.

In an old atlas he searched out the nearest railway station to Tiruvannamalai and saw that it was Tindivanam. Three rupees would suffice for the fare he thought. He wrote a short parting note and left it along with the remaining two rupees.

His letter read, "I have, in search of my Father and in obedience to his command, started from here. THIS is only embarking on a virtuous enterprise. Therefore none need grieve over THIS affair. To trace THIS out, no money need be spent. Your College fee has not yet been paid. Rupees two are enclosed herewith. Thus, _____"[11]
The letter changes from the personal "I" to the impersonal "THIS" and ends with a long line instead of a signature. From this day on he

---

[11] Narasimha Swami: Self Realization, p. 28

never signed with his name again. When he was asked later why he did not sign his letter, he answered, "There was nothing deliberate or conscious about it. Simply that the ego did not rise up to sign it."

So, at around twelve noon on this fateful Saturday, Ramana left his family and Madurai and set off to take the train to Tiruvannamalai which was approximately 250 miles away. He was never to return. The railway station was almost one mile away. According to the timetable, the train to Tindivanam left at 11.45. Though he hurried as fast as he could, he expected, of course, to be too late, but fortunately the train was also late. He bought a ticket to Tindivanam for 2 rupees 13 annas, boarded the train, and lost himself in thoughts on Arunachala. He paid no attention to either his fellow passengers or to the beautiful and varied landscape through which he travelled. A Moulavi (a Muslim well-versed in religious lore), who was sitting in his compartment, finally asked him where he was travelling. A short conversation ensued, in which he learned that there was also a railway station at Tiruvannamalai and that he needed to change trains at Villupuram.

The train reached Tiruchiappalli at sunset, and as he felt hungry he bought two of the big country pears which grow in the hilly regions of Southern India, but after the first mouthful he felt full and had no desire to eat any more. As he had always had a healthy appetite this was something quite new to him. Again he sank into a kind of waking sleep (*samadhi*) and in this way he arrived at Villupuram at around 3 a.m., where he alighted.

Having hardly any money left he decided to walk the remaining distance. At daybreak he started out to town to search for the road to Tiruvannamalai. He was too shy to ask the way, so, tired and hungry from his search, he finally entered a hotel for food. He had to wait until noon however to receive a meal. The hotel-keeper told him that Mambalapattu was a railway station on the way to Tiruvannamalai.

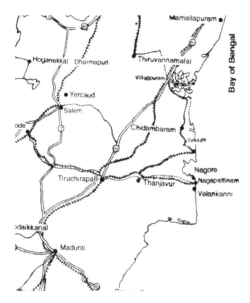

Route to Tiruvannamalai

Ramana went back to the railway station and purchased a third-class ticked to Mambalapattu, for which he had just enough money. He arrived there that same afternoon at 3 p.m.

There were still approximately 30 miles remaining, which he had to cover on foot. Under the burning August sun he presumably followed the railway track so as not to lose his way. In the evening he had covered about 10 miles and reached the temple of Arayaninallur, which is situated on a big rocky plateau. From here Arunachala is visible in the distance.

Exhausted, Ramana rested at the outer temple gate. The temple was soon opened for worship (*puja*). Ramana took his seat in the open pillared hall and sank again into *samadhi,* while the priest and the faithful celebrated the *puja*. As he sat like this a dazzling light suddenly appeared to him, flooding the whole temple. At first he thought this must be the appearance of the deity there. He rose to look in the inner sanctuary, where the image of God was situated, but all was dark there. So he found that the light had no natural origin, but, as suddenly as it had appeared, it vanished. Ramana sank back into *samadhi*. He had no idea that he was sitting next to the statue of Jnana Sambandar, one of the 63 Tamil saints. It is written that this saint, who lived in the early 7th century A.D., once saw a similar light at the same place.

Soon he was disturbed by the temple cook who wanted to lock the temple doors. Ramana asked for some food and to be allowed to spend the night there. Both were refused. The other visitors suggested that he should come with them to Kilur, a place approximately six furlongs away, where they were going to celebrate the *puja* again. There he could be given something to eat. So Ramana accompanied the group.

At the Viratteswara temple in Kilur the priest celebrated the second service of the evening together with the faithful and Ramana again sank into *samadhi*. By the time the ceremony came to an end it was already about 9 p.m. Again he asked the priest for something to eat from the offered food (*prasad*) and again his request was refused. The temple drummer, who had been watching the young Brahmin, felt sorry for him and said to the priest, "Sir, give him my share."

There was no drinking water available in the temple, so Ramana was sent to the house of a neighbouring scholar (*sastri*). He was totally exhausted and while he was waiting there for water, holding his leaf full of cooked rice, he either fell asleep on his feet or fainted and fell to the ground. Some minutes later, when he awoke, a crowd of curious onlookers had gathered round him. The rice was scattered on the dirty road. Because nothing of the blessed *prasad* was allowed to be spoiled Ramana collected each grain of it, ate, drank the water which had been brought to him and laid down on the bare ground to sleep.

The next morning, Monday 31st August 1896, Gokulashtami, Sri Krishna's birthday, one of the main Hindu festivals throughout India, was celebrated in the temples and houses of the believers. Tiruvannamalai was still around 20 miles away. Again Ramana could not find the right road and being exhausted and hungry he felt that he just would not be able to get to Tiruvannamalai on foot. He needed something to eat and some money for the train. He reflected that his gold earrings set with rubies (such earrings are worn by Brahmins) must have been worth about 20 rupees. The idea arose that he could pawn them. But how and where? Finally he went at random to the house of a man named Muthukrishna Bhagavatar and there begged for food. The dame of the house was taken with the appearance of the young Brahmin and as it was Sri Krishna's birthday she warmly welcomed the guest and served him a copious meal. Although he felt full after the first mouthful she pressed him with motherly care to eat everything.

Then Ramana asked the head of the household if he would give him four rupees in exchange for his earrings. To prevent all suspicion he found himself forced to tell him the following story - he said he was on a pilgrimage and had lost all his luggage on the way and in order to be able to continue on his travels he now needed to pawn his earrings. Muthukrishna Bhagavatar examined the earrings and finding them to be genuine gave the youth the four rupees. He noted his address on a slip of paper and asked for his address in return, then the couple asked him to stay for lunch. Ramana agreed and stayed with them until midday. The housewife gave him a packet of sweetmeats for his journey, which had been originally prepared for Sri Krishna as a food offering, but which had not yet been offered. He had to promise to come back and redeem the earrings. But as soon as he left their house he tore to pieces the slip of the paper with the address. Of whatever value the earrings might have been, there was no question of him returning for them.

As there was no train to Tiruvannamalai that day, he spent the following night at the Tirukoilur railway station near Kilur. He slept on the platform with the untouched packet of sweetmeats in his pocket. Early in the morning of the 1st September he bought a ticket to his final destination at a cost of four *annas* and a few hours later arrived at Tiruvannamalai railway station from where he walked to the holy mountain of Arunachala. He was to remain there for the rest of his life.

4. In the Arunachaleswara Temple

When Arunachala drew me up to it, stilling my mind, and I came close, I saw it stand unmoving.

Arrival in Tiruvannamalai

Arunachaleswara temple

Tiruvannamalai means 'holy mountain' (from the Tamil words tiru, meaning 'holy', and Annamalai, which is the Tamil name for Arunachala). In 1901, a few years after Ramana's arrival there, the town had a population of about 17,000. This has since grown to over 110,000.

The famous Arunachaleswara temple at the foot of the hill is 1,550 feet long and 750 feet wide and is, therefore, one of the largest temple complexes in Southern India. It dates back to the early Chola dynasty of Aditya I. and Parantaka I. (871-953 AD). It represents fire, one of the five elements, and is one of the most sacred places in

Southern India.[12] It is dedicated to Arunachaleswara, God (*Iswara*), who manifested himself as *Shiva's* column of fire in the form of the hill Arunachala (see Chapter 7).

The temple complex has three compound walls with nine gate-towers (*gopurams*) and three inner courtyards. The eastern tower, which houses the main entrance, has eleven storeys and is 216 feet high and is the second highest temple tower in Southern India. Inside the temple compound there are numerous shrines to the various gods, the impressive thousand-pillared hall with exactly 1,000 richly decorated pillars, numerous open pillared halls (*mantapas*), gardens, inner courtyards and two temple ponds.

The oldest part of the temple, the inner sanctum (*cella*), lies inside the third wall, it is square in shape and is lit only with oil lamps. This room, which only Hindus are allowed to enter, contains the holy *lingam* of Arunachaleswara. The third courtyard also contains the sanctum of the mother-goddess Unnamalaiyamma, shortened to Uma, another name for *Shiva's* consort Parvati.

When, after his three-day journey, Ramana alighted from the train in Tiruvannamalai on 1st September 1896, the holy mountain and the temple lay before him in the morning light. It is worth noting that he identified Arunachala first with the temple and only later with the mountain. Overflowing with joy he hastened to the temple, whose doors stood open as if to welcome him. He went straight to the inner shrine (*cella*) and stayed there some time in the ecstasy of complete surrender. He then left the inner temple compound and threw the unopened packet of sweets, which he had received from the Bhagavatar's wife, into the Ayyankulam temple tank.

---

[12] The other four elements are represented by the temples in Kanchipuram (earth), Tiruvanaikaval (water), Kalahasti (air) and Chidambaram (ether).

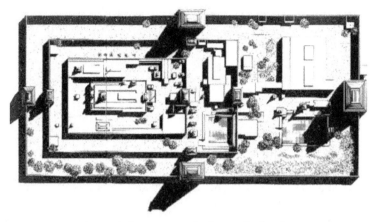

Arunachaleswara temple, isometric drawing

A man saw him do this and approached him and asked if he would like to have his tuft of hair removed.[13] Ramana agreed. One of the barbers who practised his trade at the Ayyankulam tank, cut off his beautiful black locks and shaved his head. He gave the barber some money and threw the rest of the 3 ½ rupees away. Then he tore up the *dhoti* he was wearing and kept only one piece as a loincloth. A loincloth (*koupina*) would be his only clothing from now until the end of his life. Ramana remembered an incident in his youth in Madurai concerning the wearing of a *koupina*. He told how at a festival the wife of his uncle Subba Iyer once asked him to help prepare some sweets. He hesitated and then finally refused outright, as the work would have forced him to remove his clothes and wear only a loincloth, which made him feel embarrassed. The uncle and his wife rebuked him. Ramana remarked jokingly, "If I refused to wear *koupina* once, I am now made to pay the penalty by wearing it always."

---

[13] Cutting off the tuft of hair, which orthodox Hindus have on the back of their heads as a sign of their caste, and shaving the head are signs of renunciation. Part of the formal act of starting life as a *sannyasin* is to lay down the old clothes and take a ceremonial bath.

From this day on he never touched money again and never had any possessions. Whatever he received as a gift he immediately distributed to those present. Finally, he removed his Brahmin thread, the sign of his high status.

After he had laid everything aside, he went back to the temple, without, however, taking the ritual bath prescribed by the Hindu scriptures after the head has been shaved. He saw no need for it. For quite some time there had been no rain, but now the heavens opened, so that he arrived back in the temple area drenched from head to toe and had received his 'bath' in spite of himself.

His first night in Tiruvannamalai he spent freezing in the open pillared hall in front of the temple. On the day of his arrival he had nothing to eat. Only the following day did he receive his first alms (*bhiksha*). He reports, "The next day I was walking up and down in the sixteen-pillared *mantapam* in front of the temple. Then a *Mauni* Swami [a Swami, who had taken a vow of silence]... came there from the temple. Another Palni Swami, a well-built man with long matted hair who used to do a lot of service, by clearing and cleaning the temple precincts with the help of a band of *sannyasis*, also came to the sixteen-pillared *mantapam* from the town. Then the *Mauni* looking at me, a stranger here, being in a hungry and exhausted condition, made signs to the above Palni Swami that I should be given some food. Thereupon the above Palni Swami went and brought some cold rice in a tin vessel which was all black, with a little salt strewn on top of the rice. That was the first *bhiksha* which Arunachaleswara gave me!"[14]

_____

[14] Mudaliar: Day by Day, p. 283

In the Thousand-pillared Hall and in the Patala Lingam

The thousand-pillared hall today

Ramana first settled down in the thousand-pillared hall in the temple compound, which is on the right when entering the temple through the eastern tower. The hall, with its thousand richly-carved stone pillars, is a raised stone platform, open on all sides. Here there is a constant ebb and flow of pilgrims. Exposed to the gaze of the general public in a place of pilgrimage the strange youth soon roused the curiosity of the visitors. Street urchins started to pester him. No doubt they felt provoked by a youth the same age as them, or not much older, sitting motionless like a statue in silent meditation. They used to look for him to throw stones and potsherds at him and make fun of him.

Ramana was, however, not their first victim. The ascetic Seshadriswami, who had also been living in the temple for a number of years and who was considered by people to be mad because of his often unusual behaviour, had had to endure a similar fate. As a result Ramana was also called Chinna Seshadri (the young Seshadri). But

Seshadriswami recognized in Ramana a kindred spirit, whose exceptional depth of absorption he valued. He named him Brahmana Swami (saint of Brahmins). Seshadriswami himself had renounced the world at the age of 19. He was now 26. Later he and Sri Ramana came to be known as 'the two eyes of Tiruvannamalai', whose glance sanctified the place. The bond between them lasted the whole of their lives.

Seshadriswami

Seshadri tried to protect Ramana against the attacks of the urchins, but his endeavours were unsuccessful and sometimes merely served to make matters worse.

One day, while Ramana was sitting absorbed in meditation in the thousand-pillared hall, he was pelted with stones from behind, which, fortunately, did not hit him. As a result he nevertheless decided, in order to escape such troubles in future, to withdraw to a windowless underground vault under the thousand-pillared hall, known as the Patala Lingam (patala = snakes cave, underworld, a kind of hell). There was a *Shiva lingam*, behind which he sat down, leaning his back against the wall. The cellar was never used or visited and therefore never cleaned. The rays of the sun never penetrated here. It was also damp and overrun with vermin such as woodlice, ants, bees and wasps. Despite being bitten by mosquitoes Ramana sat unmoved in yoga posture with legs crossed, impervious to the world. His thighs, where they met the ground, were soon covered with ulcers, from which blood and pus oozed. The scars were to remain visible for the rest of his life.

Here the children left him in peace. He reported, "Children used to run after me, and when I hid myself in Patala Lingam, from the outside they would pelt me with stones and potsherds, but none of it reached me as I used to sit in the south east corner. The urchins never dared to come in because of the extreme darkness that prevailed in the pit, the broken steps of which could not even be seen from the surface."[15]

A pious woman named Ratnammal found him there, she spoke to him and brought him something to eat. She urgently begged him to leave the place and come to stay at her home. But the young Swami made no reply, either through words or gestures. She laid a clean piece of cloth beside him and bade him to use it as a bed or to sit on to keep at least some of the vermin away, but he took no notice and did not even touch it. He also made no effort to obtain any food. People therefore used to place food in his mouth, but he was not aware of it. When later he was asked if he had any food during the time of his stay in the vault, he answered, "Food was forthcoming – milk, fruits – but whoever thought of food?"

Sri Ramana neither spoke nor moved. People who saw him like this thought he was practising an intense kind of spiritual exercise (*tapas*). Because he was silent, people were of the opinion that he had taken a vow of silence (*mauna*). But for him all this was no spiritual exercise at all, it was merely something that happened to him, "I have never done any *sadhana*. I did not even know what *sadhana* was. Only long afterwards I came to know what *sadhana* was and how many different kinds of it there were. Only if there was a goal to attain, I should have made *sadhana* to attain that goal.

---

[15] Bhagavan Sri Ramana, p. 29

There was nothing which I wanted to obtain. I am now sitting with my eyes open. I was then sitting with my eyes closed. That was all the difference. I was not doing any *sadhana* even then. As I sat with my eyes closed, people said I was in *samadhi*. As I was not talking, they said I was in *mauna*. The fact is, I did nothing. Some Higher Power took hold of me and I was entirely in Its hand."[16]

There is little or no information about how long Ramana stayed in *samadhi* in the Patala Lingam. It was probably several weeks. One Venkatachala Mudali, a visitor to the temple, finally brought him out of there, after Seshadri had drawn his attention to the alarming bodily condition of the young Swami. Venkatachala Mudali reports, "One day, going near the thousand-pillared hall, I found a group of boys, mostly Moslems, hurling stones in the direction of the pit. Enraged at the sight I seized a twig, and ran towards the young scamps who fled promptly. Suddenly from the dark recesses of the hall there issued forth the figure of Seshadri. I was taken aback, but, soon recovering myself, enquired of the Swami if the stones pelted by the boys had hurt him. 'Oh no,' replied the Swami, 'but go and see the Chinnaswami there', pointed towards the pit, and went away. Proceeding inside, I could make out nothing for a while, as I was coming from the glare into the darkness. In a few minutes, the faint outlines of a young face became discernible in that pit. Somewhat frightened, I went out to the adjoining flower-garden where a *sadhu* was working with his disciples. Mentioning the facts to them I took some of them with me. Even then the youthful figure sat motionless and with closed eyes, despite the noise of our footsteps. Then we lifted the Swami from the pit, carried him from the hall up a flight of steps and deposited him in front of a shrine of *Subrahmanya*. The Swami still remained unconscious, his eyes closed; evidently he was in deep *samadhi*. We noted the large number of sores on the nether side of his thighs and legs, with blood and pus flowing from some of them, and wondered how any one could remain unconscious of the body amidst such torture. Regarding it as irreverence, nay

---

[16] Mudaliar: Day by Day, p. 274

impertinence, to make any further noise in such presence, we bowed and came away."[17]

In Different Areas of the Temple Compound

At the shrine of *Subrahmanya* there lived a *Mauni* Yogi and a group of mendicant ascetics, who had settled down in the nearby garden. Sri Ramana was cared for occasionally but not regularly. At noon each day the Yogi used to bring him a glass of milk collected from a stone basin after the sacrifice to the statue of Goddess Uma. This was no pure milk, but a murky mixture of various food offerings - milk, water and sugar mixed with turmeric powder, raw and ripe pieces of plantains and other sacrificial remains, which the priest had poured over the devotional image. Indifferently Ramana swallowed it all. When the temple priest who performed the service at Uma's shrine, noticed that one day, he was dismayed. He thereafter arranged that pure milk without any additions be brought to Ramana as soon as it had been offered to the Goddess.

During this time any food had still to be put into his mouth, as he would not eat what was merely placed in front of him. Without the care of others the Swami would probably not have survived for long.

After spending some weeks at this shrine Ramana moved to the adjoining flower garden. Tall oleander plants grew in this garden, some of them ten or twelve feet high and he would sit here in their shade, deep in *samadhi*. At times he would sit down under one tree only to find himself, when he later opened his eyes, sitting under another tree. He also often did not know whether it was day or night, "When I closed my eyes, deeply absorbed in meditation I hardly knew whether it was day or night. If at any time I opened my eyes I used to wonder whether it was night or day. I had no food and no sleep. ... If there is no movement, you do not need sleep. Very little food is enough to sustain life. That used to be my experience.

---

[17] Narasimha Swami: Self Realization, p. 48

Somebody or other used to offer me a tumblerful of some liquid diet whenever I opened my eyes. That was all."[18]

Some people, who saw the young ascetic sitting motionless like that thought, "He is sitting like a Jada (dull-witted person); he must be a mad fellow." Ramana later said that he found such remarks amusing and wished that everybody could be overcome by such 'madness'.

Finally, Ramana moved to the hall where the vehicles for the temple processions were kept (vahana *mantapam*). Here he was again exposed to the pestering of the street urchins and therefore withdrew into the dark, inside the hall under the vehicles. Again he sometimes found himself under a different vehicle from the one he had sat down under. Somehow he had managed to clamber over all the obstacles without being hurt and without being roused from his *samadhi*.

After some time Ramana left the vahana *mantapam* and sat under the Illupai tree which was inside the outer wall of the southern temple tower. The path used for the temple processions passed nearby. At *Kartikai,* in particular, large numbers of pilgrims would pass by.

Here Ramana was fully exposed to the weather. Sometimes a cold wind blew and his body would be covered with dew. To protect himself against the cold he would cross his arms about the upper part of his naked body. Later he reflected that no woollen blanket could compare to the arms laid across the chest and that this was the first upper garment that he used.

He even reported that he had been naked at times. "It was not because I had a *vairagya* [renunciation] that I should have no clothing of any sort. The cod-piece I was wearing used to bring on sores where it touched the skin. When the sore became bad, I threw away the cod-piece. That is all. There used to be an old *Gurukkal*

---

[18] Nagamma: Letters, p. 175

[temple priest] who for the first time arranged for some regular food for me either by supplying some from his house or by sending the *abhisheka* milk [sacrificed milk] from the temple to me. After I had been nude for about a month, this old *Gurukkal* told me one day, 'Boy, the *Kartikai Deepam* is approaching. People from all the 24 districts will be flocking here. Police from all the districts will also be here. They will arrest you and put you into jail if you are nude like this. So you must have a cod-piece.' So saying, he got a new piece of cloth, made four people lift me up and tied a cod-piece round me."[19]

At the following *Kartikai* festival Sri Ramana's first disciple, Uddandi Nayinar, arrived and became a permanent companion. He had a bullock cart which he used to transport people and goods from one town to another. Like so many other pilgrims he too had come to Tiruvannamalai for the *Kartikai* festival and saw the young Swami sitting under the Illupai tree absorbed in deep *samadhi*. In search of Self Realization and peace of mind he recognized in the young Swami the living embodiment of the Holy Scriptures and said to himself, "Here indeed are Realization and peace, and here must I seek them." From then on he did not leave his side. He took care of his bodily needs and prevented him from being disturbed or bothered. He settled down at a short distance from him, observed the crowds of visitors for hours at a time and drove away the urchins who found it amusing to cause trouble for the young ascetic. He also cooked simple meals, which he shared with him.

Uddandi was a learned man. In Sri Ramana's presence he recited sacred Yoga and *Vedanta* texts such as *Yoga Vasistha* and *Kaivalya Navaneeta*. He longed to hear some words of instruction from his new guru, which would help him on the way to Self Realization and help him find peace, but the Swami kept silent and he, in his turn, did not dare to speak to him.

---

[19] Mudaliar: Day by Day, p. 283

Uddandi was unable to remain with Ramana constantly. During his lengthier absences Ramana was again pestered by street urchins or people who were curious to see him. Here there were no dark places where he could hide. Many thought him simply to be a lazy good-for-nothing and played tricks on him. One day, while he was sitting under the Illupai tree in *samadhi,* unaware of his body, when no-one was near, a boy poured some mud over his back to find out how deep the absorption of the young ascetic was. When Ramana later came back to body-consciousness he noticed that his loincloth was wet and stinking and that someone must have played a prank on him. He did not feel any anger, but the time was approaching when he would leave the temple area and move to a quieter place.

5. In the Small Temple of Gurumurtam and in the Mango Grove

If one realizes one's true nature within one's heart, it is the plenitude of being-awareness-bliss without beginning or end.

Gurumurtam

It was because of Uddandi Nayinar that Annamalai Tambiran first noticed Ramana. Tambiran used to wander about accompanied by a crowd of followers singing sacred hymns from the *Tevaram*. He collected alms, fed the poor and served at the tomb of an *adina-guru* at the small temple of Gurumurtam near the village of Kilnathur, one of the eastern suburbs of Tiruvannamalai. One day, as he was walking past the Illupai tree he saw the young Swami sitting there and was deeply impressed, from that day on he accompanied Uddandi Nayinar. Finally they both suggested to Sri Ramana that he should move to Gurumurtam. There he could meditate undisturbed as the place was secluded and in addition offered better protection from the cold. Ramana agreed and in February 1897, not quite six months after his arrival at Tiruvannamalai, he left the temple area and was brought to Gurumurtam by Tambiran and Uddandi.

45

At times Tambiran, due to his devout but excessive veneration, became a nuisance to Sri Ramana. One day he made preparations to render homage to his new guru like to one of the idols of the goddesses in the temple (*abhishekam*). He obtained flowers, oil, sandal paste, milk and other ingredients and actually wanted to pour this over the head of his "living god". To prevent this, Ramana took a piece of charcoal and the next day, before Tambiran arrived, wrote on the wall in Tamil, "This [food] alone is the service [needed] for this [body]."

When Tambiran arrived with his meal, Ramana pointed to the written words on the wall, then to the food as "this" and on himself as the (second) "this". So Tambiran was forced to abandon his plan. Through this incident people learned that the silent Swami was educated and able to read and write.

Amongst the admirers who had started to visit Ramana regularly, was a highly-placed official called Venkataramana Iyer. When he realized that the Swami was able to write, he felt he must find out his name and where he came from. But Ramana, despite repeated questioning, remained silent. Iyer finally explained that he would not leave until his questions were answered, even if that meant that he would have to go hungry and get into trouble because of his lengthy absence from his office. This moved the young Swami and he wrote down the words, "Venkataraman, Tiruchuli". The place, however, was unknown to the official. So Ramana reached for the *Periyapuranam*, which was lying at his side, and pointed out Tiruchuli as the name of a village, whose temple was honoured in the famous hymn by Sundaramurti (one of the 63 Tamil saints). Thus, not only the official but Tambiran and all those present discovered his name and his origins. From now on Ramana was no longer nameless and unknown.

Ramana was absorbed in deep *samadhi* most of the time unaware of his body, which he neglected, completely disregarding his outward appearance. He was filthy, his hair had grown very long and had become a dishevelled and matted mass and his fingernails had grown so long and crooked, that he was unable to use his hands for any useful purpose. Neither Tambiran nor Uddandi did anything about this and he himself felt no need to change his bodily condition. Only later, when Palaniswami took care of him, did the daily bath become a routine.

Once, however, he was forced to bathe and on another occasion to have a shave, "Even so, a lady, by name Minakshi, who used now and then to bring food to give me, one day brought a large pot and began to boil water. I thought it was for some use for herself, but, taking from a basket some oil, soap-nut, etc., she said, 'Swami, please come'. I did not move. But would she keep quiet! She pulled me by the arm, made me sit, smeared the oil all over my body and bathed me. The hair on the head which had got matted for want of care, was now spread out and hung down like the mane of a lion. ... Shaving was also like that. The shave I had on the day I came here has been recorded; the second was after a year and a half. The hair had got matted and woven like a basket. Small stones and dust had settled down in it and the head used to feel heavy. I had also long nails, and a frightful appearance. So people pressed me to have a shave, and I yielded. When my head was shaven clean, I began to wonder whether I had a head or not, it felt so light. I shook my head this way and that to assure myself that it was there. That showed the amount of burden I had been carrying on my head."[20]

About an unsuccessful attempt to shave him, when he was still living at the *Subrahmanya*-shrine, he reported, "One Nilakanta Iyer ... used to come there frequently. One day, he came prepared for the purpose. Thinking that he had come as usual, I kept my eyes closed. Without saying a word to me, he stood some way off opposite me. I heard a 'tip, tup' behind me, so opened my eyes. I saw a barber sharpening his razor. I left the spot immediately without saying a word. Poor man, he realized that I was not willing to be shaved and so had gone off."[21]

---

[20] Nagamma: Letters, p. 305f
[21] dto.

The place where Ramana sat was infested with ants, but he took no notice of them as they crawled over his body and bit him incessantly. After a while his devotees sat him on a stool against the wall. To keep the ants away they placed the legs of the stool in jugs of water, but to no avail, as the ants merely ran up the wall and bit his back. To this day the imprint of his back can be seen where he sat leaning against the wall.

Nor did Ramana react to outer events or threats. Once thieves came into the garden at Gurumurtam to steal tamarinds. When they noticed the young Swami sitting under one of the trees and not paying the least attention to them, one of them said to the others that he would trickle the caustic juice of a plant into his eyes to see if that would make him react. But Ramana remained unmoved. Finally they gave up their plans and vanished with the fruits of their labour.

Day by day Sri Ramana's fame grew. People flocked to admire this extreme example of self-denial. Some said, "This Swami must be very old", and pointed to his long fingernails. They thought that he had used yoga to keep his body young, but that, as his nails had grown so long, he must actually be very old. Others were convinced that with so much saintliness he could fulfil all their wishes for prosperity, health, children and, of course, salvation from the cycle of rebirth. They therefore laid offerings at his feet and sang his praises. The result of all this was increasing disturbance for him, so that eventually a bamboo fence was constructed around him for his protection.

During the first two months spent in Gurumurtam, Tambiram used to give him some of the food which had been offered at the Gurumurtam shrine. But then Tambiran went away, after first asking Uddandi to look after the Swami. He promised to be back in a week but, in fact, only returned a year later. Some weeks after he left, Uddandi also had to return to his own *math*. So suddenly no one was there to care for Ramana. But, as a result of his increasing fame, food was always brought to him. After the departures of both Tambiran and Uddandi the only problem was that there was no-one there to keep the crowds away. This problem was finally solved when Palaniswami joined him.

Palaniswami was a Malayali from Kerala and at least 20 years older than Sri Ramana. He paid homage to the idol of Goddess *Ganesha* in a temple in the town. His only food was food which had been offered to *Ganesha*, which consisted of a single meal a day, to which he added no spices, not even salt. Someone noticed his devotion to the Goddess and said, "What is the use of spending your lifetime with this stone Swami? There is a young Swami in flesh and blood at Gurumurtam. He is steeped in austerities (*tapas*) like the youthful Dhruva mentioned in the *puranas*. If you go and serve him, and adhere to him, your life would serve its purpose." Others also drew his attention to the fact that the Swami was without an attendant at the time and that it would be a blessing to serve such a great soul. Spurred on in this way Palaniswami went to Gurumurtam.

When he saw the young Swami, he recognized that he had found his master. He continued with his service at the *Ganesha* temple for a while, but after some time he gave it up. He became a devoted companion of Sri Ramana following him everywhere like a shadow. If he had to leave he used to lock the door at Gurumurtam, so that nobody could pester the Swami while he was away, and he would always return as quickly as he could. Nobody was allowed to see Ramana without his permission. He would accept the various food offerings from visitors, mix them up into a paste and at noon give Ramana a cupful of it to eat. The rest he gave back as *prasad* to the visitors. This single meagre meal was just enough to survive on. Ramana's body became as thin as a skeleton.

In addition, as he was permanently seated and never made the slightest movement, he had barely enough strength to maintain his sitting posture and was severely constipated. If he needed to rise to relieve himself, which was sometimes after days only, he found it very difficult, repeatedly falling back in his seat. Incapable of keeping himself upright he would stagger to the door. When one day

Palaniswami held him up by his arms, Sri Ramana reproachfully asked with signs, why he was holding him, and Palaniswami answered, "Swami was about to fall, and so I held him and prevented the fall." He himself had not even noticed the fact.

Some time in May 1898, after a little over one year spent at Gurumurtam, Ramana and Palaniswami moved to the adjoining mango grove. Here they spent several peaceful months undisturbed by the numerous visitors, as Venkataraman Naicker, the owner of the garden, let no-one enter who had not been asked in. There they lived in two narrow sheds under a mango tree. Ramana remembers, "Under a mango tree they erected something overhead to prevent rain from falling on me. There was, however, not enough space under it even to stretch my legs fully while sleeping. So I used to sit almost all the time like a bird in its nest. Opposite my shelter Palaniswami also had a small shed. In the huge garden, only two of us used to stay." [22]

Palaniswami, who had access to a library in town, brought back a number of books in Tamil on *Vedanta*, such as *Kaivalya Navaneeta*, *Yoga Vasistha* and *Shankaras Vivekachudamani*. But, as his knowledge of Tamil was not very good, he used to struggle through the scriptures word by word and often had difficulties in understanding. Ramana read each of the books, immediately grasped the meaning, remembered everything and imparted the essence of it to Palaniswami. In this way Ramana gradually learned about all the important *Vedanta* scriptures and discovered that his personal experience corresponded with them. The experience he had had on the upper floor of his uncle's house in Madurai was exactly the same as the experiences he found described in the scriptures.

---

[22] Bhagavan Sri Ramana, p. 35

6. Sri Ramana's Steadfastness

Silence is unceasing eloquence. It is the best language.
There is a state when words cease and silence prevails.

Ramana's disappearance and his parting note were soon noticed. His family was stunned. His mother Alagammal, who was living in Manamadurai, was informed and every effort was made to try and find him. But nobody, neither friends nor neighbours, had any idea where he might be. People hoped for his return, but in vain, as weeks and months went by without any news. Alagammal's anguish increased and she beseeched both her brothers-in-law, Subba and Nelliappa Iyer, to try and find him. It was rumoured that Ramana had joined a theatrical troupe performing religious dramas in Trivandrum. Nelliappa Iyer twice went there to look for him among the various troupes, once accompanied by Alagammal – but without success.

Almost two years went by and people started to believe that they would never see the lost son again. On 1st May 1898 Subba Iyer died. Nelliappa Iyer and the rest of the family came to the funeral in Madurai. During the funeral a young man from Tiruchuli brought the unexpected news that he had met Tambiran and had heard him talking about a young Swami, called Venkataraman, who came from Tiruchuli. The Swami was a venerated saint in Tiruvannamalai and was undoubtedly the person they were looking for.

Immediately after the funeral Nelliappa Iyer and a friend started out for Tiruvannamalai. There they learned that the young Swami was living in the mango grove. However, when they went there they were prevented from entering by the owner of the garden, who said that Ramana was a *mauni*, a silent saint, and should not be disturbed. Nelliappa Iyer therefore wrote the following message on a piece of paper for his nephew, "Nelliappa Iyer, pleader of Manamadurai, wishes to have your *darshan*", and asked Naicker, to pass on the message.

Ramana recognized his uncle's handwriting. The piece of paper came from a records office and had on the back some official entries in the handwriting of his older brother Nagaswami. From this he was able to conclude in addition that Nagaswami had become an employee in a records office. He agreed that his uncle should enter.

When Nelliappa Iyer saw his unwashed nephew, with his unusually long fingernails and his unkempt hair, he was seized by the contradictory feelings of pleasure at seeing him and concern about his physical condition. As he regarded him as a *mauni* he did not speak to him directly but said to Palaniswami and Naicker, that it was a great joy to see a family member in such a high state of development. Nevertheless the welfare of the body should not be totally neglected. His family would certainly have no desire to make him give up his vows and lifestyle, but they would like to have him near them in Manamadurai so that they could care for him. He could live there undisturbed as an ascetic and *mauni* at the shrine of a great saint. All his wants would be seen to. Nelliappa Iyer argued and pleaded with all the eloquence of a lawyer. But Ramana did not move and gave not the least sign of recognition.

The uncle finally had no alternative but to give up. He sent Alagammal the joyful news that he had found her son, but that he had changed a lot and sadly would not return. Nelliappa Iyer himself returned to Manamadurai after five days, unsuccessful in his mission.

About his two uncles, Nelliappa and Subba Iyer, Sri Ramana later remarked, "Subba Iyer had great courage and pride, but this man [Nelliappa] was very meek and mild. If it had been Subba Iyer, he would never have gone back home leaving me here. He would have bundled me up and carried me away. As I am destined to stay here, my whereabouts were not known so long as he was alive. … Nelliappa Iyer, being spiritually minded and mild in his ways, left me here saying, 'Why trouble him?'"[23]

---

[23] Nagamma: Letters, pp. 358 ff

Later, Nelliappa Iyer visited his nephew twice while he was living in the Virupaksha cave. Ramana had by then started to give spoken answers to his disciples' questions and to interpret the holy *Advaita* scriptures. Once, whilst he was in the midst of an explanation about the *Dakshinamurti Stotram,* his uncle unexpectedly came to visit and was astounded by his nephew's erudition. From that day on Nelliappa knew that he need not trouble himself anymore and returned home deeply satisfied. Soon afterwards he died.

A few months after Nelliappa's first visit, Sri Ramana left the mango grove to live in a small temple in Arunagirinathar. He had decided that he should no longer be dependent upon the care of others and that from now he would look for his own daily meal. So he said to Palaniswami, "You go one way, beg your food and get on. Let me go another way, beg my food and get on. Let us not live together." But Palaniswami, in the evening returned to the Arunagirinathar temple, saying, "Where can I go? You have the words of life." Now Ramana felt compassion for him and Palaniswami was allowed to stay with him.

After they had spent about four weeks during August and September 1898 living in the small temple, they went to live for a week in the quiet upper rooms of the towers of the Arunachaleswara temple and in the Alari garden, one of the temple gardens. There Ramana was again tracked down by admirers. He withdrew from them and went to Pavalakkunru, one of the eastern foothills of Arunachala where there was a *Shiva* temple, a cave and a spring. He sat most of the time in *samadhi* in a tiny room in the temple, which was so small that it was impossible to stand upright. Several times, after performing the *puja,* the priest forgot to see if the Swami was sitting in his room and inadvertently locked him in.

His admirers also tracked him down in Pavalakkunru. Patiently they waited until he appeared from inside the temple or the cave to have his *darshan.*

Once the following amusing incident happened, "They bolted the door on the outside when they went into town for food, fearing that Bhagavan might slip away. He, however, knew that the door could be lifted off its hinges and opened while still bolted, so in order to avoid the crowd and the disturbance he slipped out that way while they were gone. On their return they found the door shut and bolted but the room empty. Later, when no one was about, he returned the same way. They sat telling one another in front of him how he had disappeared through a closed door and then appeared again by means of *siddhis* (supernatural powers), and no tremor showed on his face, though years later the whole hall were shaking with laughter when he told the story." [24]

In the meantime Ramana had decided to look for his own food and used to go into town to beg for his meals. About the first time he went begging he said, "The first day, when I begged from *Gurukkal's* wife, I felt bashful about it as a result of habits of upbringing, but after that there was absolutely no feeling of abasement. I felt like a king and more than a king. I have sometimes received stale gruel at some house and taken it without salt or any other flavouring, in the open street, before great pandits [scholars] and other important men who used to come and prostrate themselves before me at the Ashram."[25]

When Ramana went begging in the evenings he used to stand at the doors of the houses and clap his hands. He received the food in his hands and ate it standing on the street. He never took more than two or three handfuls. He also never entered a house, even if he was invited. As the young Swami was by now famous in Tiruvannamalai and people hoped that he would come to their doors, he used to choose a different street each day to avoid disappointing anyone. Later he said that he had begged in all the streets near the temple.

During the Christmas holidays of 1898 his mother came to visit him for the first time, accompanied by her eldest son Nagaswami, who

---

[24] Bhagavan Sri Ramana, p. 39
[25] Mudaliar: Day by Day, p. 207

had a few days off work. They had searched for him in the mango grove in vain. Now they had climbed up to Pavalakkunru. Ramana was laying on a rock in a state of neglect such that he was barely recognizable, clothed in a dirty scrap of a loincloth only. Twenty-eight months had passed since his mother had last seen him. Bitterly she complained about his neglected bodily condition and implored him to come home with her, but he did not react.

Day after day they came up to see him, brought him sweets and entreated him tirelessly, but all to no avail. Ramana remained silent. Alagammal tried everything. One day when she broke down in tears, he was unable to bear it any longer and simply went away.

Once she despairingly turned to the others present and asked for their support. Then one of them said to Ramana, "Your mother is weeping and praying. Why do you not answer her? Whether it is 'yes' or 'no', why not give her a reply? Swami need not break his vow of silence. Here are pencil and paper. Swami may at least write out what he has to say." So Ramana wrote down, "The Ordainer controls the fate of souls in accordance with their past deeds – their *prarabdhakarma*. Whatever is destined not to happen will not happen, - try how hard you may. Whatever is destined to happen will happen, do what you may to stop it. This is certain. The best course, therefore, is for one to be silent."[26]

Whether this message convinced his deeply religious mother or not, there was nothing left for her to do but to leave him to the life he had embarked upon. Furthermore Nagaswami's holidays were coming to an end and he had to return to his office. Without having achieved what they had set out to achieve and with a heavy heart, they returned to Manamadurai.

---

[26] Narasimha Swami: Self-Realization, p. 66

7. Sri Ramana and Arunachala

That is the holy place. Of all, Arunachala is the most sacred. It is the heart of the world. Know it to be the secret and sacred Heart-centre of Shiva.
(from the Arunachala Puranam)

Arunachala, the Holy Hill

Arunachala, situated in the wide plain of Southern India, is considered to be a holy hill and one of the most sacred places in India. It has been venerated for many thousands of years. From time immemorial ascetics and saints have lived in the many caves on the eastern slope of the mountain.

The Sanskrit name Arunachala means red mountain (aruna = dawn, also the colour crimson; achala = hill, also the immovable). Figuratively 'aruna' also stands for the liberated state which is beyond the opposites, 'achala' stands for the immovable, for stability and silence. Arunachala is the centre where all forces are in balance, a place of harmony. It is reported that *Shankara* said that Arunachala is mount Meru, which, according to Indian mythology, is the axis of the world, the centre of the universe and the dwelling place of the Gods. Ramana also interpreted Arunachala as *sat-chit-ananda* (being-consciousness-bliss).

Geologically Arunachala is an isolated massif of volcanic rock in the Eastern Ghats. It is older than the Himalayas and therefore the oldest natural shrine on earth. Although only 2,682 feet high it dominates the landscape for miles around. Various medicinal plants grow on its slopes. During the monsoon, from July to November, violent rivers of rainwater flow down the hill, whereas from April to June everything is dry.

In the past, particularly on its northern and southern slopes, Arunachala was covered in woods and inhabited by wild animals such as tigers, panthers and snakes of all kinds. But even during the time the Maharshi was living there, little remained of this original flora and fauna. The foot of the hill retained a small jungle inhabited by various rodents, lynx, jackals, snakes and of course large numbers of monkeys.

Today Arunachala is suffering an environmental crisis, with increasing water pollution in the many water tanks, the unauthorized building of huts and houses, the noise of loudspeakers and increasing amounts of traffic. The wood has almost completely disappeared, with only a few bushes and shrubs remaining. Climate change has meant that the rainfall has decreased. As a result, a few years ago, a reforestation and environmental protection project was set in motion.

The Mythology

Deepam

In the Arunachala Puranam, which forms part of the Skanda Puranam, there are several legends about the origin of the holy mountain. The following is the most widely known - *Vishnu* (the Preserver) and *Brahma* (the Creator) were arguing about which of them was the greater. Their argument brought chaos on earth, so much so that the gods begged *Shiva* to intervene as mediator in the dispute. Consequently, *Shiva* manifested himself as a column of light from which his voice could be heard, saying that the one who could reach either the upper or lower end of the column, would be declared the greater. *Vishnu* took the shape of a boar and dug himself deep inside the earth. *Brahma* took the shape of a swan and soared into the air to reach the upper end. When he saw the blossom of a mountain tree floating through the air, he brought it to *Shiva* saying that he had found this on the summit of the column, hoping to win by deception. *Vishnu*, however, being unable to reach the lower end of the column, and as he recognized the highest light shining within himself, as it shines in the hearts of all creatures, lost himself in meditation. He became unconscious of his physical body and forgot himself and that he was seeking the bottom of the column of light. When he returned to *Shiva*, he confessed his failure and praised him with the words, "You are Self-knowledge. You are OM. You are the beginning, the middle and the end of everything. You are everything and illuminate everything." He was thereupon recognized as the greater. *Brahma,* ashamed, had to admit his attempted deception and *Shiva* forgave him.

The story ends stating that, because the column of light was too bright, *Shiva* chose to manifest himself as mount Arunachala during the months of *Kartikai* (November/December). Arunachala therefore is regarded as adi-*lingam*, the first *lingam*, i.e. the first manifestation of *Shiva*, the Highest Lord, the God of all Gods and the true and absolute Self.

This legend is the basis for the annual festival of *Kartikai Deepam* in November/December. It is one of the oldest festivals in India and is mentioned in Tamil scriptures dating back 3,000 years. It is celebrated over ten days and culminates on the last full moon night with the festival of lights (*Deepam*). At six o'clock in the evening the image of Arunachaleswara is carried out of the temple in a procession. At the same moment a giant flame is lit using camphor and clarified butter *(*ghee) – *Shiva* in the form of a column of fire. For the flame nearly 1,000 kilograms of ghee are poured into an enormous vessel. The wick consists of a piece of cloth several metres long. In the dark evening sky the flame is visible in the surrounding plain over 20 miles away. For several days the flame is kept alive. Everyone who sees the flame on Arunachala considers it to be a manifestation of *Shiva*. It symbolizes the fact that whoever recognizes the light of all lights, which shines in his own spiritual Heart, and meditates upon it without interruption, obtains final Liberation (*moksha*).

Circumambulation of the Holy Hill (Pradakshina)

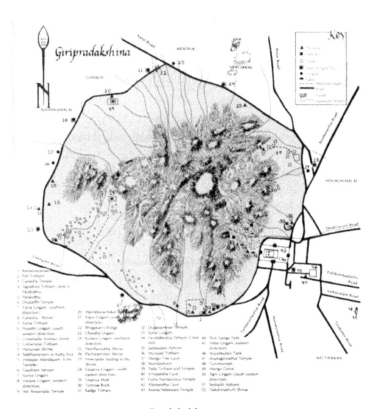

Pradakshina route

One of the favourite means of expressing devotion to the hill is by walking round it - *giri-pradakshina* (*giri* = mountain; *pradakshina* = circumambulation). The ritual circuit round an object, a person or a temple is a customary act of worship in Hinduism. As Arunachala is the manifestation of Lord *Shiva* himself and therefore a holy mountain, its circuit has always been regarded as a most important spiritual exercise which sets the mind to rest, helps to attain liberation and the forgiveness of sins and even grants worldly wishes. In the Arunachala Puranam there are several instructions for carrying out the circumambulation on foot, which is recommended to all pilgrims. The traditional circuit is approximately 8 miles long and leads clockwise round the hill.

Milestones, some of them 700 years old, mark the way. Part of the path passes through the town of Tiruvannamalai and on the way one comes across numerous water tanks (*teerthams*), *lingams,* shrines and temples such as the Adi Annamalai temple, the shrine of Manikkavasagar and the Durga temple. The Arunachaleswara temple, Esanya *math* and the Ashram of Seshadri Swami are also on the path. There is also a shorter inner circuit of about 6 miles.

According to tradition the pilgrim moves barefoot and as slowly as a pregnant queen would walk. He/she walks in silence or sings pious songs or recites a *mantra*. Some days are more popular for *pradakshina* and on these days devotees flock to Arunachala in great numbers. *Deepam*, the night during *Kartikai* when the sacred flame is lit on the top of the hill, is the most popular. Thousands go round the hill that night. Full moon nights are also popular for *pradakshina*.

Sri Ramana often practised this form of devotion and recommended it to his devotees. He gave the following interpretation for this form of meditation, "*Pradakshina* (the Hindu rite of going round the object of worship) is 'All is within me.' The true significance of the act of going round Arunachala is said to be as effective as circuit round the world. That means that the whole world is condensed into this Hill. The circuit round the temple of Arunachala is equally good; and self-circuit (i.e., turning round and round) is as good as the last. So all are contained in the Self. Says the *Ribhu Gita*: 'I remain fixed, whereas innumerable universes becoming concepts within my mind, rotate within me. This meditation is the highest circuit (*pradakshina*)."[27]

---

[27] Talks, p. 178 (from Talk 212)

Usually Sri Ramana and his companions would go around the hill at night, returning in the early hours of the morning. Later it became customary for visitors to assume responsibility for the food (*bhiksha*) for the day for the small number of Ashram occupants that there were at the time, five rupees being more than enough. Afterwards they would go with Ramana round the hill at night.

The following day everyone took a nap to make up for the sleep they had missed, everyone except Ramana that is. He was not allowed to sleep, as visitors were constantly dropping in. If a new visitor came and spent his *bhiksha* and asked Maharshi to go round the mountain with him in the evening, he would say to his companions, "Poor man! He had come all the way from a long distance to do *giri pradakshina* with me. That is why he offered *bhiksha*. If you told him that I had gone round the hill for three days, he would definitely not allow me to do so tonight. Yet, in his heart of hearts he would be disappointed." So it happened, that Ramana did not sleep for two or three nights. If he was asked, if the sleepless nights did not affect him, he would reply, "What is sleep? It means resting the mind. But it is only when you have a mind that you need to rest it. However, to be awake all night will bring eye-strain and eye-ache, naturally. But, if you close the eyes and remain quiet for some time, the eye-strain will go; that is all! Then, where is the problem?"[28]

When people from town learned that Sri Ramana had again started out on *pradakshina* and would be passing by the town, they would come out to bring him something to eat or to express their feelings of veneration for him. So if he came near Esanya *math* and the town, he would send his companions ahead. Kunju Swami reports, "So, after sending all the others off, he would cover himself with a shawl and reach the Ashram by a by-path. ... If we went round the hill at night, he would, on nearing the town, ask us not to sing or talk loudly as that might disturb the people in their sleep."[29]

In 1926 Ramana suddenly stopped going round the hill, although he continued with his regular walks. The cause was a dispute between his younger brother Nagasundaram, who had by now come to live with Ramana, and Narayana Rao, one of the Ashram occupants. Narayana Rao had to stay behind to deal with the kitchen work, while all the others went around the hill, which was not to his liking. When Ramana heard about the argument, he said, "There is a controversy because I go round the hill. You please go round the hill without me." He said these words calmly but firmly. After this incident he never again went round the hill.

Another reason why Ramana gave up the circumambulation of the hill may also be the fact that the number of visitors had increased enormously. He wanted to be available to all who came to him and he could not accept that newcomers should be forced to wait for his return. He was always keen to avoid troubling or disappointing people. So he now restricted himself to his simple walks.

Sri Ramana encouraged everyone to do *pradakshina*, even people who did not believe in the effectiveness of this long walk. He once said to his devotee Devaraja Mudaliar, "For everybody it is good to

---

[28] Ganesan: Moments, p. 62
[29] Nagamma: Letters and Recollections, p. 14

make circuit of the hill. It does not even matter whether one has faith in this *pradakshina* or not just as fire will burn all who touch it whether they believe it will or not, so the hill will do good to all those who go round it. … Go round the hill once. You will see that it will attract you."[30]

Sri Ramana's Relationship with Arunachala

All his life Sri Ramana referred to the spiritual effect of the mountain. Once when he was asked why he had left his home and come to Arunachala, he answered that he had been drawn there by Arunachala itself. The force could not be denied. "Arunachala is within and not without. The Self is Arunachala." Another time, when he was asked about the nature of Arunachala he answered, "For the human eye it is only a form of earth and stone but its real form is Jyoti [divine light]."

There are innumerable other examples which could be quoted, in particular his five hymns in praise of Arunachala, but there is one thing that cannot be denied - if Ramana can be said to be emotionally attached to anything it was to Arunachala.

Sri Ramana also often stated that the mountain is inhabited by supernatural beings (*siddhas*), who live on the hill in various forms, even as animals and who at times come into contact with human beings. It is also reported that Ramana had several visions concerning Arunachala. This may seem strange, as in general he accorded no significance to visions. Nevertheless he did have them and spoke of them occasionally. As Major Chadwick writes, "Bhagavan … would sometimes tell us that he had seen inside the hill a great city with large buildings and streets. It was all very mysterious. There he had seen a big company of *sadhus* chanting the *Vedas*, most of the regular devotees were among the company, he said, and he saw me there. 'But that's only a vision,' someone

---

[30] Mudaliar: Recollections, p. 65

remarked, 'All this is only a vision too,' he would reply, meaning our world. 'That is just as real as this.'"[31]

Ramana's sketch of Aruanachala and Tiruvannamalai

In the end Sri Ramana's relationship with Arunachala is something which only can be hinted at, but not grasped. His verses to Arunachala whilst being spiritual love poems of enormous emotional depth are also teachings of great wisdom. They are some of the most valuable scriptures which he left. At the hour of his death, on 14th April 1950, devotees sang verses from his poem to Arunachala 'Akshara Mana Malai' (The Marital Garland of Letters). When he heard the singing, tears welled up in his eyes. He died at 8.47 p.m. and at that precise moment a bright shooting star, visible for miles around and seen by hundreds of people, moved slowly towards Arunachala. Whatever meaning is attached to this event, one thing is certain, Sri Ramana was, and still is, united with Arunachala, the hill of the divine light, which for him was nothing other than the Self, "The mystery of this hill is the mystery of the Self."

---

[31] Sadhu Arunachala: Reminiscences, p. 57. The Arunachala Puranamam also tells of invisible saints living inside the hill.

8. In The Virupaksha Cave

Sivaprakasam Pillai: "Swami, who am I? And how is salvation to be attained?"
Sri Ramana: "By incessant inward enquiry 'Who am I?' you will know yourself and thereby attain salvation."

The Simple Life in the Virupaksha Cave

The tomb of Virupakshadeva today

Soon after his mother and his brother returned home Sri Ramana left Pavalakkunru and moved up the hill. He lived for a short time in the Satguru Swami Cave on the south-eastern slope, then in the Namasivaya Cave. He finally settled down in the Virupaksha Cave, where he remained from 1899 to 1916.

The Virupaksha Cave is quite large and is about 330 feet above the Arunachaleswara temple on the south-eastern slope. The inner part of the cave contains the remnants of the Saint Virupakshadeva, who performed severe acts of penance there in the 13th century.

At the time Ramana took up abode there nobody felt responsible for the Virupaksha *math* and the cave was empty. There was a lawsuit in progress between two different groups, who both claimed possession of, and the income from, the *math*. But as no decision had yet been made, nobody was caring for it. The issue of possession was, in fact, only resolved some years later. At the following *Kartikai* festival the successful litigants came up to the cave and started charging a fee to visit it. So access to the Swami who lived there suddenly became conditional upon payment of a fee, although he himself was not informed of the matter. As large numbers of people were now coming up to see him, quite a few had to go away disappointed when they were told they had to pay.

When Ramana heard about this practice, he left the cave and sat down under a tree. Those collecting the fees then declared this place also to be an outer area belonging to the *math* and continued to demand money from all those who wanted to approach him. He had no alternative, therefore, but to go away again. At first he lived in the Satguru Swami Cave which was lower down, then in another cave, consequently the Virupaksha Cave was no longer a source of revenue. The owners of the cave finally understood that they could not misuse the young Swami for their own purpose, so they gave up the fees they had collected and asked him to continue to live in the cave. As a result Ramana returned and stayed there until 1916.

In winter Virupaksha was a fine lodging, but not so in summer, when the adjoining riverbed dried up and there was not the slightest breeze. In addition, as there were almost no trees, the cave was exposed to the sun, so that it became unbearably hot.

A little higher up the hill, at the foot of a mango tree there was a cave known as the Mango Tree Cave. The nearby Mulaipal

Teertham always had a supply of clean water. The first time Ramana had seen it, it had been uninhabitable. But since then two brothers had removed the overhanging rock, had built a small wall with a door and had made the cave inhabitable. They asked the Swami to use it, so he used to spend the summer months here.

Ramana at the age of 22

Life at the Virupaksha Cave and Mango Tree Cave was rich in privations but carefree, as Ramana himself stated, "Palaniswami asked me to copy out and give him some stanzas of *Shankara*, but where were notebooks or paper with us at the time? I collected every scrap of paper I could, stitched them together into a notebook, wrote out the stanzas and gave them to him. At that time we had nothing but a pot; we did not have even a towel. In the early days of our stay in the Virupaksha Cave, Palaniswami alone had a towel to wrap around him. The cave had no iron doors then; it had a wooden door with a wooden latch. We would fasten it from the outside with a small stick, go around the hill, wander hither and yon, return after a week or ten days, then open the door with the help of another stick. That was our key at the time; no need to keep it anywhere! This notebook was the only article we took with us. As Palaniswami wore a towel, he used to fold the book and tuck it into his waist. That was enough for us."[32]

Years later this outer poverty had hardly changed at all. It is reported that Ramana had a single towel which was full of holes and which he used both to dry himself after his bath and for the kitchen work. He used to hide it carefully so that nobody would catch sight of it. One day, however, when, despite his efforts, it was discovered, his followers at once started to look for some new towels.

His loincloth was also in a poor state, "My *koupina* got torn. I do not usually ask anyone for anything. Bodily privacy has however to be maintained. Where could I get a needle and thread available to mend the *koupina*? At last, I got hold of a thorn, made a hole in it, took out a thread from the *koupina* itself, put it into the hole and thus mended the cloth, and, so as to hide the place where it was mended, I used to fold it suitably before putting it on. Time passed like that. What did we need? Such were those days!"[33]

Sri Ramana never wore shoes, not even during the hottest months. Rangan, a former classmate, reports, "When Bhagavan and I climbed up to the top of Arunachala, a thorn pricked my foot. Noting that I was lagging behind, Bhagavan removed it. A few yards later a big thorn pricked his foot. When I looked at his foot there were so many unremoved thorns in it. Then I examined the other foot, but the position was not different. 'Which one will you remove, the new thorn or the old ones?', he queried. He broke the thorn by pushing his foot to the ground and started walking again."[34]

There was no cooking in the Virupaksha Cave. Visitors used to bring milk, fruits, cake and other food. Gradually more followers

---

[32] Bhagavan Sri Ramana, p. 47
[33] Nagamma: Letters, pp. 50ff
[34] Unforgettable Years, p. 43

came to live with Ramana and Palaniswami. Any food donated was always evenly distributed. But as it was not possible to rely on sufficient food for all being brought by visitors, Palaniswami and other devotees would go down to the town to beg for additional food. Then Ramana would mix up all the food donated, make a mash by pouring hot water over it and gave each one a glassful. Often there was not even any salt to flavour it, but Ramana thought it better to be without than to beg anyone for it, "If once we begin to ask for salt, we would feel like asking for *dhal*, and when we ask for *dhal*, we would feel like asking for *payasam* and so on. So we felt that we should not ask for anything, and swallowed the gruel as it was. We used to feel extremely happy over such diet."[35]

Devotees asked Sri Ramana, to compose a hymn to sing during the regular begging tours in town. So the famous 'Akshara Mana Malai ('The Marital Garland of Letters', which is contained in 'The Collected Works') came into being. It is a deeply spiritual and heart-moving hymn in praise of the much loved hill Arunachala, which the devotees now sang on their begging tours. Ramana remarked humorously, "'Marital Garland of Letters' fed us for many years."

The begging mission to town followed a fix course. At least four of Ramana's devotees started on their way, announcing their arrival to the inhabitants by blowing their conches. They then went through the streets singing and collecting what was given to them.

As for kitchenware there was only one earthen pot, later there was an aluminium pot, then one of brass. The pots grew in number. When Ramana's mother joined the community in 1916 she instigated regular housekeeping chores and regular cooking. But Ramana made it clear in several remarks that he preferred the simplicity of the years when they lived from hand to mouth.

Some days there was not enough of anything, on other days there was more than enough eatables. At times Ramana, so as not to

---

[35] Nagamma: Letters, p. 85

disappoint anyone, ended up overeating. There is a well-known story of how one day he planned a day of fasting and started off early in the morning to walk alone on the hill. There he met several women who competed with each other to serve him food. He had to eat all that they served him. Some hours later he met them again and again they forced him to eat. Then he lay down in a *mantapam* to sleep. In the evening he wanted to return to the Virupaksha Cave when a devotee met him, bringing him mangoes cooked in *rasam*. He ate this too. Jokingly he said, "It is like the story of the man who fled the town of mice and found himself in the land of tigers."

Sometimes people would also send their carriages to pick him up for a meal. But he always refused, as he feared that if he accepted there would be no end to the invitations.

The First Works Come into Being

Various people used to come up the hill to see the young Swami - the curious, the educated, who only wanted to test his knowledge, and spiritual seekers. Simple folk, children, even animals, all would come. Increasingly visitors with spiritual questions came to have their doubts cleared and to have spiritual scriptures explained. Ramana would write the answers down on little scraps of paper or on a slate using a piece of chalk, as at the time he was not talking.

One of Ramana's earliest disciples was Gambhiram Seshayya who worked as a Municipal Office Overseer at Tiruvannamalai. He was studying the teachings of Vivekananda on different yoga techniques such as breath control, *raja-yoga* and *jnana-yoga*. As there were parts he did not understand he used to bring his books and explain his difficulties. Ramana glanced over the books and answered the questions by writing down the essence of the teachings in simple Tamil on small scraps of paper. So, over time, Seshayya found himself the owner of a large bundle of scraps of paper covering the years 1900 - 1902. He copied the answers given into a small notebook.

When Seshayya died in the late twenties, the booklet was found in his belongings. His elder brother made it available to Ramanashram. It was eventually published as the earliest work of Sri Ramana with the title 'Vichara Sangraham' (Self-enquiry), which is also included in 'The Collected Works'.

Another of Sri Ramana's disciples was Sivaprakasam Pillai, a philosopher, who was employed in the Revenue Department. In the many books he had studied he could not find the answer to his existential quest "Who am I?". In 1902 he came to Tiruvannamalai for the first time on official duties. He heard about the Swami on the hill, visited him and asked him the burning questions that were troubling him. Again the answers were written down by Ramana on the floor or with chalk on a slate. Afterwards Sivaprakasam Pillai made notes of the questions and answers from memory. In 1923 he published them under the title 'Nan Yar' (Who am I?), which is again found in 'The Collected Works'.

'Nan Yar' starts with the following introduction, "As all living beings desire to be happy always, without misery, as in the case of everyone there is observed supreme love for one's self, and as happiness alone is the cause for love, in order to gain that happiness which is one's nature and which is experienced in the state of deep sleep where there is no mind, one should know one's Self. For that, the path of knowledge, the inquiry of the form 'Who am I?' is the principal means."[36] In the following passage Sri Ramana explains in greater detail what is meant by the quest and how it should be undertaken (see also Chapter 18).

What was explained by Sri Ramana to his early disciples in his first works, when he was barely more than twenty years old, has remained unchanged over the years. Above all 'Nan Yar' contains the essence of what Ramana taught throughout his life. When newcomers used to arrive at Ramanashram and ask him about his

---

[36] Collected Works, p. 39

teaching, he would point to this booklet. He insisted that it should be sold so cheap that even the poorest could afford it.

It must be stressed that Ramana himself never felt moved to formulate his teaching of his own accord, either verbally or in writing. His writings – of which there are few – came into being as answers to questions asked by his disciples or through their urging, with the exception of a few hymns, which were his own initiative.

Ganapati Muni

Ganapati Sastri, also called Ganapati Muni – Muni means the wise, the scholar, the saint – was the most famous and erudite of Sri Ramana's disciples. He hailed from Andhra Pradesh and was a Brahmin. In his youth he had already written literary works and could speak and write Sanskrit fluently at the age of fourteen. When he was 22 he took part in a meeting of learned Sanskrit scholars and writers, he was awarded the title Kavya-Kantha (one from whose throat poetry arises spontaneously) because of his virtuosity in poetical improvisation.

In 1903 he came to Tiruvannamalai for the first time to practise intense *tapas* (spiritual ascetic exercises). He stayed for one year and during that time he twice visited the Swami, who was approximately the same age as himself. On both occasions his erudition was noticed. Finally he took up the post of school teacher at Vellore. But it was the renewal of India which was closest to his heart and to which he devoted most of his energy. Through intense *tapas*, in particular through *mantra japa,* he believed he would obtain the energy required to achieve this goal. He dreamed of an ideal society based on the *Vedas*, in which there would be material prosperity and social justice as well as spirituality. He used to hold long public discourses on this theme and soon gained a circle of followers.

In 1907 he resigned his position as teacher in Vellore and returned to Tiruvannamalai at the time of the *Kartikai* festival, in order to practise *mantra japa* more intensely. He was driven by a deep dissatisfaction about his knowledge and abilities and overcome by gnawing doubt. He had achieved nothing concrete, despite the numerous extreme spiritual exercises and sacrifices he had performed and his intense study of the Holy Scriptures. He was unsure if he had understood the essence of the scriptures at all and if his *tapas* was correct. Then he thought of the Swami.

Ganapati Muni

It was on the ninth day of the *Kartikai* festival, 18th November 1907 at about half past one, when, in the midday heat, he climbed up the hill to the Virupaksha Cave. He was trembling with emotion. The young Swami was seated alone in front of his cave. Although, because of the festival, there were crowds of people everywhere, there was nobody at all near the Swami. Even Palaniswami was not there. Ganapati Muni fell prostrate on the ground, grasped Sri Ramana's feet with both hands and uttered trembling, "All that has to be read I have read. Even *Vedanta Sastra* [the holy scriptures of *Vedanta*] I have fully understood. I have performed *japa* to my heart's content. Yet I have not up to this time understood what *tapas* is. Hence have I sought refuge at thy feet. Pray enlighten me about the nature of *tapas*."

Ramana and Ganapati Muni

For 15 minutes the Swami kept silent and looked at Ganapati, who sat at his feet full of expectation. Then he answered, "If one watches whence this notion of 'I' springs, the mind will be absorbed into that. That is *tapas*. If a *mantra* is repeated, and attention directed to the source whence the *mantra*-sound is produced, the mind will be absorbed in that. That is *tapas*."[37]

This was the first time that Sri Ramana gave a verbal answer to a question. Until then he had kept silent and had always written the answers down. It is remarkable how he led the *mantra* practice of his new disciple back to the method of Self-enquiry. For Ganapati

---

[37] Narasimha Swami: Self Realization, pp. 89ff
The source of the mantra is not primarily the vocal organs, but rather the mind, which creates the idea of the sound and whose source is the Self.

Muni this was a real revelation. His heart was filled with ecstatic joy and he meditated at the feet of his new master until the evening.

The following day Ganapati Muni wrote full of enthusiasm to his family and his disciples, "I have found my Master, my Guru. He is the Sage of Arunachala known as Brahmanaswami. He is no ordinary Swami. He is a great Seer, a mighty spiritual personality. To me and to you all he is Bhagavan Sri Ramana Maharshi [elevated great Seer Ramana]. Let the whole world know him as such."[38]

From that moment on the Swami became known as the Maharshi, Bhagavan or simply Ramana. Ganapati Muni and his followers made Sri Ramana known to a wide circle in India.

At first Ganapati Muni stayed with the Maharshi and lived close by in the Mango Tree Cave, where he practised his *tapas*. Over the next three weeks, to express his gratitude, he wrote a hymn of 1000 verses in praise of the Goddess Uma or *Shakti*, the divine mother of the universe, whom he venerated above all others.

From January to March 1908 he stayed with Ramana and a number of disciples in the Pachaiamman temple. There the recently finished masterpiece of 1000 verses to Uma (Umasahasram) was solemnly recited.

Ganapati Muni strove earnestly to deepen his meditation and to practise Self-enquiry, as the Maharshi had taught him. But he still believed in his mission to renew India and also in the effectiveness of *mantra japa*. So, he once again felt restless and drawn to leave. At the end of March he went to Sri Ramana and asked him in parting, "Is the seeking of the source of 'I' thought, sufficient for the accomplishment of all my aims, or is *mantra* dhyana [*mantra* meditation] needed?" Ramana answered, "The former would suffice." Then he gave him the following advice for his future life, "Place your burden at the feet of the Lord of the universe who is

---

[38] Shankaranarayanan: Bhagavan and Nayana, p. 5

ever victorious and accomplishes everything. Remain all the time steadfast in the heart, in the Transcendental Absolute. God knows the past, present and future. He will determine the future for you and accomplish the work. What is to be done will be done at the proper time. Don't worry. Abide in the heart and surrender your acts to the Divine."[39]

First Ganapati Muni returned to Tiruvottiyur near Madras, where he used to live. There the world of learning reserved for him an enthusiastic reception. Then he withdrew to the Ganapati temple to practise his spiritual exercises, where he one day had a strange experience. It was the eighteenth day of his *tapas* when he had a vision of the Maharshi, who suddenly came in, sat near him and placed his hand on his head. He felt a strong stream of energy flooding through his body. It is interesting that at the same time Ramana also had a strange experience, which he later described to Ganapati Muni as follows, "I lay down, but I was not in *samadhi*. I suddenly felt my body carried up higher and higher till all objects disappeared and all around me was one vast mass of white light. Then suddenly the body descended and objects began to appear. ... The idea occurred to me that I was at Tiruvottiyur. I was on a high road which went along. On one side and some distance removed from it was a Ganapati temple. I went in and talked, but what I said or did, I do not recollect. Suddenly I woke up and found myself lying in Virupaksha Cave."[40]

Ganapati Muni spent his whole life moving around and was often accompanied by his wife Visalakshi, who also led a spiritual life. At many places he gave lectures about Sanskrit literature and explained his ideas on social reforms (which he considered to be very progressive), gave interpretations of the *Vedas*, spoke about spiritual matters and was invited to various events, as he was very much in demand as a speaker. But again and again he would withdraw to Tiruvannamalai for short periods. On these occasions he would

---

[39] dto., p. 14
[40] Narasimha Swami: Self Realization, pp. 94ff

mostly live in the Mango Tree Cave, where he performed *tapas* and visited his master frequently.

During his absence he wrote letters to the Maharshi, which testify to his deep devotion. On 31st March 1931 he said in his letter from Sirsi, "Boongiver! Though I may have a thousand desires, they all are set at rest within the cave of the Heart scorched by the effulgence of your benevolent look. Only one of them sprouts forth raising its head even now. Let my impure ego perish. My Lord, grant me the fulfilment of my aspiration." And on 14th April 1931 his letter ended as follows, "I know that the perfect fulfilment of all my aspirations is to be accomplished only at the proximity of Bhagavan's Feet. I am awaiting that auspicious hour. For the present, may this devotee, staying at some distance, appear very near to Bhagavan's Heart. Lord you reside within my heart and I at your Feet. You are my Master and Director. I am your servant, your instrument to do your work."[41]

The relationship between them remained close all their lives. Sri Ramana called Ganapati Muni by the pet name Nayana, which his disciples also used. The Telugu word Nayana is used to address one's father as well as one's disciple and one's child.

In return Ganapati Muni's erudition made much literature, in particular Sanskrit literature, accessible to the Maharshi. Ramana relied totally upon Nayana in the matter and finally himself started to learn Sanskrit by reading *Shankara's Vivekachudamani* in Tamil and Sanskrit in parallel. In 1915 he wrote his first verse in Sanskrit. This verse contains the essence of his teaching and was included in Ganapati Muni's 'Ramana Gita', "In the interior of the Heart-cave *Brahman* alone shines in the form of the *atman* with direct immediacy as I, as I. Enter into the Heart with questing mind or by diving deep within or through control of breath, and abide in the *atman*."[42]

---

[41] The Guru and the Disciple, pp. 26 and 28
[42] Sri Ramana Gita, p. 11.

Two years later Ramana composed his 'Five Stanzas to Sri Arunachala' (Arunachala Pancharatna) in Sanskrit. In 1927 he rendered his own work of 30 verses Upadesa Undiyar (The Essence of Instruction) into Sanskrit as Upadesa Saram. He sent his translation to Ganapati Muni to be checked and corrected and Ganapati wrote a commentary on it. Upadesa Saram is one of the most important of the Maharshi's works. Ramana also translated it into Telugu and Malayam. His famous 'Reality in Forty Verses' (Ulladu Narpadu) is also one of his most important works and was translated into Sanskrit by Ganapati Muni. Again the English translations can all be found in 'The Collected Works'.

Ganapati Muni died in 1936, aged 58, in Kharagpur, West-Bengal, where his devotees had built an ashram for him. When Ramana was informed about his death by telegram, he said, deeply moved and with tears in his eyes, "Where can we find another like him?"

Children, Devotees and Visitors

Though Sri Ramana did not speak in the first years of his stay in the Virupaksha Cave, many children climbed up the hill to visit him. They came on their own initiative and sat silently near him for long periods. They often used to bring something to eat with them and he also received his share. Sometimes they brought their dolls and played at weddings. For the yearly light festival (Dipavali) they brought crackers and Ramana set them off together with them. He also played marbles with the boys.

In the meantime many new followers had joined Sri Ramana. Amongst them was Echammal, a simple woman, who had lost her husband and both her children, which had made her life unbearable. Someone told her that a young saint was living in Tiruvannamalai. She immediately undertook the journey to see him. She stayed in his

---

In the Ramana Gita, the famous teaching poem, which Ganapati Muni wrote upon the model of the *Bhagavad Gita*, he gives the Maharshi's answers to his disciples, classified by theme.

presence for about one hour, without a word being spoken. She felt the mental anguish vanishing until the pain disappeared, to be replaced by inner peace. She settled down in Tiruvannamalai and took a vow that she would only eat after she had served her master. From 1907 onwards until her death in 1945 she brought him a meal every day.

Entrance to Virupaksha Cave today

In 1908, as a boy of twelve, T.K. Sundaresa Iyer had come to Ramana and remained faithful to him till the end. He writes in his reminiscences, "Had you seen him in those days, you would hardly have taken him for a mere human being. His figure was a statue of burnished gold. He simply sat and sat, and rarely spoke. The words he spoke on any day could easily be counted. He was an enchanting personality, who shed a captivating lustre on all, and a life-giving current flowed from him, charging all those nearby, while his sparkling eyes irrigated those around him with the nectar of his Being."

And yet one day the young man was finally overcome by doubts. "One day I wondered why I was visiting him at all. What was the use? There seemed to be no inner advancement. Going up the hill was meaningless toil. I decided to end my visits on the hill. For one hundred days exactly I did not see Bhagavan. On the hundred and first day I could suffer no longer and I ran to Skandashram, above Virupaksha Cave. Bhagavan saw me climbing, got up and came forward to meet me. When I fell at his feet, I could not restrain myself and burst out in tears. I clung to them and would not get up. Bhagavan pulled me up and asked, 'It is over three months since I saw you. Where were you?' I told him how I thought that seeing him was of no use. 'All right,' he said, 'maybe it is of no use, so what? You felt the loss, did you not?' Then I understood that we did not go to him for profit, but because away from him there was no life for us."[43]

Frank Humphreys

The Englishman Frank H. Humphreys was the first western disciple who came to Ramana, in January 1911. He reports about his visit, "For half an hour I looked Him in the eyes which never changed their expression of deep contemplation. I began to realize somewhat that the body is the Temple of the Holy Ghost – I could only feel His body was not the man, it was the instrument of God, merely a sitting

---

[43] Iyer: At the Feet, pp. 17 and 3ff
The episode happened when Sri Ramana was already living in Skandashram.

motionless corpse from which God was radiating terrifically. My own sensations were indescribable."[44]

The story of how Sri Ramana kept his identity hidden from a visitor is well-known. One day when Palaniswami was not there, Sri Ramana started to build a stone platform in front of Virupaksha Cave, so that visitors could sit there more comfortably. He collected some stones and bricks and mixed some wet mud. He had a bricklayer's trowel in his dirty hand, was wearing only a loincloth and was sweating when a visitor came. He asked him where the Swami was. But Ramana answered, "Swami has just gone out somewhere." The visitor waited, but as no Swami returned he went away without having achieved what he had come for. On the way back he met Echammal, who was on her way up to the cave to bring the meal. She told him, that he had come across none other than Ramana himself. Later Echammal asked Ramana if it was right for him to give the visitor such wrong information, but Maharshi replied, "Do you want me to go about with a bell round my neck announcing 'I am the Swami' or to have a label on my forehead that I am the Swami?"

There are other similar incidents, in which Ramana denied himself.

Sannyasins and Sadhus

In people's eyes Sri Ramana led the life of a *sannyasin*, but he never had any formal initiation. Once a disciple of the present Shankaracharya of Sringeri[45] tried to persuade Ramana to be initiated into *sannyasa*. Ramana refused. But the *sannyasin* was stubborn, arguing for more than three hours. Then he went away to get all the things needed for performing the ceremony of initiation saying Ramana should think it over in the meantime. Shortly after the *sannyasin* left, an old man, who Ramana had never seen before,

---

[44] Humphreys: Glimpses, p. 15
[45] In Sringeri in the South *Shankara* founded his first monastery. The Shankaracharya is the head of the monastery following a strict line of succession.

came to the Virupaksha Cave carrying a bundle of Sanskrit books. The old man asked permission, to leave the books there for a while and to pick them up later on his way back. Ramana leafed through them with interest. The first book he picked up was the Arunachala Puranam. It fell open at the following verse, "Those who reside within the radius of three yojanas (30 miles) of this place [Arunachala], even if they have not had initiation, shall by my supreme decree attain Liberation, free from all attachments." He copied this out on a slip of paper, laid the book back and closed his eyes. When he later looked up the books had disappeared. Finally the *sannyasin* returned. Sri Ramana gave him the piece of paper and he was forced to accept that for Maharshi no initiation was needed.

Some of the other *sadhus* who lived on the mountain, watched Sri Ramana's increasing fame with suspicion and envy. An elderly *sadhu* felt particularly envious and wanted to drive Ramana out of the Virupaksha Cave. He threw some rocks over a ledge at the young Swami sitting under it, but they missed. When the *sadhu* tried it again, Ramana got up and caught him. But the *sadhu* only laughed and said that it was meant only as an innocent joke. Without rebuking him Ramana let him go.

A certain Balananda was particularly intrusive. One day he said to Ramana, "I will say I am your Guru and get money from the visitors. It is no loss to you so don't contradict me." Ramana did not reply and when visitors came, Balananda said to them, "This young Swami is my disciple. Yes, give the child some sweets."

Once Balanada sat beneath Ramana and gazed steadily into his eyes in order to put him into nirvikalpa *samadhi* (*samadhi* without bodily awareness). But all that happened was that Balananda fall asleep, Ramana got up and went away with his disciples.

At the Tortoise Rock

Tortoise Rock (Foto: R. Clarke)

In 1912 Ramana had a kind of second death experience. One morning, around 10 a.m. he was on his way back from the temple tank at the Pachaiamman Shrine together with his companions Palaniswami, Vasudeva Sastri and others. There they had taken an oil bath. The sun was by now burning hot and the ascent to Virupaksha Cave was causing additional strain. When they came near the Tortoise Rock, which is a huge boulder on the path, Ramana was suddenly overcome by a bodily weakness. He supported himself against the rock. His skin turned dark and his companions thought he was going to die.

Vasudeva Sastri reports, "While all else stood at a distance weeping, I suddenly embraced him. I was a bachelor at the time and had the liberty to do so. No one else used to touch Swami's body. He was in that state for about ten minutes, I think, and then gained consciousness. I jumped about with joy. 'Why this weeping? You thought I was dead? If I am to die, will I not tell you beforehand?' Bhagavan said, consoling us."

Ramana described his experience as follows, "Suddenly the view of nature in front of me disappeared and got covered up like a sheet of white cloth. ... All around me was the view of the white cloth. My head was reeling. The circulation of blood and the beating of the heart stopped, and my body began to get dark in colour, same as what happens to a dead body, and as that slowly increased, Vasu thought that I was really dead and began to weep, and embraced me. The change in my body's colour, Vasu's embrace, the shivering of his body, and the talks of the others around me – I was conscious of all these. I was also conscious of my hands and feet getting chill, and the stopping of the beats of my heart, but I had no fear in me. The flow of my thoughts and the consciousness of my self were not lost and I was not worried about my body's condition. I sat cross-legged in the padmasanam pose [lotus seat]. I was not leaning on the rock behind. The circulation of blood stopped but the sitting posture remained intact. All that lasted for about fifteen minutes. Suddenly energy permeated throughout my body. The circulation of blood and the beating of the heart commenced. The black colour of my body disappeared. I began to perspire profusely from all pores in my body. I opened my eyes, got up and said: 'Come on. Let us go.' We then reached the Virupaksha Cave without any further incidents."[46]

It is possible that this event allowed Ramana's final transition to a normal outer life. One thing is certain, around this time his life started to follow a normal path again. This development had been gradual and had started to set in in the years leading up to this event. He had started to react to visitors and had slowly started speaking again, although still very little. He ate and drank regularly and took care of his body. He performed all kinds of domestic work. He also carved many walking sticks, which he then gave away, and likewise spoons and cups which he carved out of coconut shells and then

---

[46] Both reports in: Nagamma: Letters, pp. 121ff

polished so long that they started to shine. He developed a good deal of practical ability in daily life, became an extraordinarily good and painstaking cook, a talented architect and in all that he did was extremely economical and tidy. Increasingly his life followed a precise timetable, in which everything had its fixed place.

9. At Skandashram

A visitor asked, "I am a man with a family. Is it possible for those in a family to get release, and if so how?"
Maharshi, "Now what is family? Whose family is it? If the answers to these questions are found the other questions solve themselves. Tell me: Are you in the family, or is the family in you? Who are you?"

Alagammal

Sri Ramana spent the years 1916 to 1922 with his mother Alagammal and the small community at Skandashram. It was during this period that he was joined by a number of those disciples who were to remain with him permanently, these included Viswanatha Swami, Ramaswami Pillai and Kunju Swami. His younger brother Nagasundaram also joined the Ashram. When Alagammal died in 1922, she was buried at the foot of the hill. Shortly thereafter the time at Skandashram came to an end, as the Maharshi and his followers moved to settle down at her burial site, and Ramanashram, where Sri Ramana was to remain until his death, came into being.

The Mother is Reunited with her Son

It was not until 1913, fifteen years after her first visit, that Alagammal finally saw her son again. She came to see him on her way back from a pilgrimage to Benares, bringing with her Mangalam, the wife of her youngest son Nagasundaram. Both were allowed to stay at Virupaksha Cave for one night, which was the first time that any women had spent the night there. Alagammal prayed to her son for his blessings for Mangalam, in particular that her wish for a son would be fulfilled. Then both women returned to Manamadurai.

Shortly afterwards Mangalam became pregnant and gave birth to a son, who, in gratitude to Ramana, was named T.N. Venkataraman (also to be known as Venkatoo).[47]

In 1914 Alagammal made a second pilgrimage. On the way back she again went to see Ramana. During her visit she became seriously ill with a high fever that lasted several weeks. The symptoms pointed to typhus. When her state became critical, Ramana wrote a passionate prayer to Arunachala pleading for her recovery. This prayer is the only one in which he begged Arunachala to heal someone and to intervene in someone's fate. The last strophe runs as follows,

---

[47] T.N. Venkataramam was now the only direct descendant of Sundaram Iyer's family. After the death of his father Nagasundaram (Chinnaswami) he became the Ashram President in 1953.

"Arunachala, that chasest away illusion (*maya*)! Why delayest Thou to dispel my mother's delirium! Besides Thee, is there anyone who with maternal solicitude can protect the suppliant soul and ward off the strokes of destiny?"[48]

Alagammal subsequently recovered and later returned home.

As a result of several deaths in her family and the difficult circumstances of her life Alagammal finally felt that she should spend the remaining years of her life with her second son. Nagaswami, her eldest son, had died in 1900. Soon after her visit to Ramana her brother-in-law Nelliappa Iyer had died and then also her daughter-in-law Mangalam. The house in Tiruchuli had been sold to cover debts. Nelliappa Iyer had left the family in difficult circumstances.

In early 1916 Alagammal set off for Tiruvannamalai. As she did not know whether she would be allowed to stay with Ramana in the Virupaksha Cave she moved in with Echammal, who each day brought a meal up to the cave. But after some time she felt the urgent need to stay with her son. The community, however, did not want to see any change in the established Ashram routine. Without consulting Ramana they declared with one voice that under no circumstances should women be allowed to live in the cave. Although the other women argued that the mother should be permitted to do so as she was now too old to climb the hill each day, they remained unmoved. When Sri Ramana came to hear about the matter he at first kept silent. Alagammal stood there unhappy and despairing and wanted to go, when Ramana, deeply moved, took her hand and said, "Come let us go, if not here we can stay somewhere else, come." Fearful that he may indeed go away they all immediately changed their view and Alagammal moved into the Ashram.

---

[48] For the Mother's Recovery. In: Collected Works, p. 149

Life at Skandashram

Skandashram today

At the Virupaksha Cave there was often not enough water or at times none at all. But further up the hill there was a waterfall under which the members of the community took their daily bath. Alagammal, however, was too old to climb up to the spring. Ramana told how he used to fetch the water for her 'bath' from this spring in two *kamandalams*, "I used to bring water in both of them, carrying one in each hand. She used to sit down wearing a small cloth and I used to pour the water over her head just as we do *abhishikam* over an idol. That is how she used to have her bath. ... Someone used to wash her cloth and bring it back. That was all. If water was brought in those two *kamandalams* all her requirements used to be met."[49]

Kandaswami, one of Sri Ramana's disciples, eventually found this all too tiresome. Also, because of the growing number of disciples, the Virupaksha Cave was becoming crowded. He therefore decided to look for another place to stay, where they could live more

---

[49] Nagamma: Letters, p. 381

comfortably and he thought that the best thing would be to settle down at the spring. Once Ramana had given his agreement, he started work, cleared away the undergrowth, cacti and trees, removed the rocks and started building the Ashram. He also planted a garden with coconut trees. Ramana named the new Ashram after him. Kanda is the Tamil name for *Skanda*, and so the new lodging was named 'Skandashram'. It is one of the most enchanting places on the hill with an impressive view of the Arunachaleswara temple and the whole town.

More and more people were coming to Sri Ramana. Swami Thapovan Maharaj reports about his visit, "One midday I, a young *brahmachari* at that time, climbed to the cave, saw the Maharshi there and placing a bunch of bananas at his feet, bowed and sat before him. At the same moment some monkeys jumped on the scene, scrambled for the fruits and ran away with them. Maharshi looked lovingly into my face. That was all. He spoke but Silence; not a word passed between us. A supreme, a dynamic and divine Silence prevailed. An hour passed by, all in Silence. He rose for his *bhiksha*. I too rose from my seat, bowed again and walked down the hill. The divine Silence sank deeper and deeper into me at each step!"[50]

Viswanatha Swami, who became a lifelong disciple of Ramana, reported about his first visit to him, "My first *darshan* of Bhagavan Sri Ramana was in January 1921, at Skandasramam, which is on the eastern slope of Arunachala and looks like the very heart of the majestic hill. It is a beautiful quiet spot with a few coconut and other trees and a perennial crystal-clear spring. ... His look and smile had remarkable spiritual charm. When he spoke, the words seemed to come out of an abyss. One could see immaculate purity and non-attachment in him and his movements. I sensed something very refined, lofty and sacred about him. In his vicinity the mind's distractions were overpowered by an austere and potent calmness and the unique bliss of peace was directly experienced.

---

[50] Swami Thapovan Maharaj: The Soul of Silence. In: The Mountain Path, 1986, p. 135

This I would call 'Ramana Lahari', 'the blissful atmosphere of Ramana'. In this ecstasy of grace one loses one's sense of separate individuality and there remains something grand, all-pervading, all-devouring."[51]

The daily routine at Skandashram was subject to strict regulation. At four o'clock in the morning Alagammal would rise and sing devotional songs, while the other community members meditated. Then Akshara Mana Malai (The Marital Garland of Letters) was recited. Afterwards Ramana took his bath. To brush his teeth he sat on a big stone slab on the eastern side of Skandashram. He continued to do this even when the weather was cool, nobody could make him give this up. Exactly why he did so was only discovered later. An old woman was in the habit of coming up daily for *darshan*. When her health would no longer allow her to climb up the hill, she could see Ramana from her house when he brushed his teeth at this place. He knew how important this was for her, so he always sat there, irrespective of the weather.

At eight there was *rasam* and rice for breakfast. After this the Ashram community sat outside. Some devotees read, others meditated. The atmosphere was very peaceful. Occasionally Ramana answered the questions of devotees and visitors.

In the evening Akshara Mana Malai was recited again. Ramana would close his eyes and sink into meditation. Sometimes his meditation was so deep that great efforts were needed to bring him back to normal consciousness. Someone would then blow into a conch to wake him up.

When Alagammal moved into Skandashram, food was meagre and depended upon whatever visitors and devotees brought. Sometimes the food was delicious and there was more than enough for everybody, at other times there was much less and sometimes nothing at all.

---

[51] Natarajan: Timeless, pp. 173ff

Soon Alagammal started cooking regularly and took charge of running the household. She would wander about the hill and bring back things that she found there. She was an excellent and imaginative cook and liked to spoil the devotees with a variety of delicious dishes, using the ingredients she had somehow managed to find.

In 1918/1919 Tiruvannamalai was devastated by plague. It was at this time that Kunju Swami joined the Ashram, in a very bizarre manner. He became a close companion of Sri Ramana and remained at the Ashram after the death of Maharshi, where he himself died in 1992. Many episodes from Ramana's life have been reported through him. When he came to Ramana, the town was deserted because of the plague and only a few people had remained at the Ashram. Annamalai Swami, who was attending Sri Ramana at that time (not to be confused with the other Annamalai Swami, who later directed the building work at Ramanashram) died because of it.

Ramanatha Brahmachari was also infected. One day Ramana and some devotees were going round the hill and decided to rest at Pachaiamman temple. One of them said, "We shall all remain here, since Ramanatha Brahmachari is afflicted with the plague. Arrangements can be made to send food to Skandashram." When Ramana heard this, he was outraged, "What a wonderful idea! He came to me as a boy with complete faith in me. Is it proper for me to stay here leaving him alone there? If you are afraid of the plague, you may all stay here. I will go and stay with him. When you bring food to him, you can bring some to me also."[52] When they heard this, they all fell silent embarrassed. Ramanatha Brahmachari soon regained his health and no-one caught the plague from him.

---

[52] Kunju Swami: Reminiscences, pp. 18ff

Alagammal's Last Years

During her last years Alagammal still had some lessons to learn. When she first came to live with Ramana he did not call her 'Amma' (mother). Sometimes he would ignore her and not answer her when she spoke to him, whilst at the same time paying attention to everybody else. If she complained he would say to her, "All women are my mothers, not only you." This was very hurtful for her. At first this would often make her cry, but later she learned to give up the possessiveness she felt towards her son and to overcome any feelings of superiority she may have had at being the mother of the great Swami.

Sometimes Ramana made fun of her strict orthodox way of living. Though meals at the Ashram were strictly vegetarian, Alagammal also thought, as do very orthodox Brahmins, that certain plants were impure ('unsattvic'), for example onions. One day Ramana said to her jokingly, "Amma, what are you going to eat? Today they have brought only drumsticks [a kind of vegetable] and onions. If you eat them, will you not encounter forests of drumsticks and mountains of onions on the way to *moksha*?"[53]

Gradually Alagammal came to see that for the spiritual path only moderation in food was required. If by accident her sari were to touch a non Brahmin he would tease her, saying, "Look! Purity is gone! Religion is gone!" But little by little her strict opinions concerning caste weakened.

If Alagammal were to think that this thing or that thing were needed, Ramana would say to her, "Mother, if you want bodily comfort, go to the other son; if you want mental comfort you stay here." Alagammal understood and became accustomed to the life of privation at the Ashram. She never thought of leaving.

---

[53] Natarajan: Bhagavan Ramana and Mother, p. 25. Strict orthodox Brahmins consider onions to be impure food, as they are said to arouse passions.

She once wanted to prepare appalams for her son (thin crispy cakes made with dark flour), as he used to like them very much. In secret she went to various people to beg for the ingredients and in the evening, when all the visitors had left, she was ready to start preparing the appalams. She wanted to make between two and three hundred of them so she asked Ramana to help her, as he used to do as a boy. But he refused saying, "You have renounced everything and have come here, haven't you? Why all this? You should rest content with whatever is available. I won't help you. I won't eat them if you prepare them. Make them all for yourself, and eat them yourself." But she did not give way. Then he had another idea, "All right. You make these appalams. I will make another kind." And he started to compose a song about appalams. Alagammal knew several similar *advaitic* songs, such as the rice song and the soup song, but so far there was no appalam song, and she liked this kind of song. So, while she was preparing the appalams he wrote the song and both finished their work at the same time. The last verse runs as follows,

"Put the appalam in the ghee of *Brahman*
Held in the pan of infinite silence
And fry it over the fire of knowledge.
Now as I transmuted into That,
Eat and taste the Self as Self,
Abiding as the Self alone."[54]

Alagammal wanted her younger son Nagasundaram, whose wife had died, to come to live with them in the Ashram. His sister Alamelu had taken over the upbringing of his small son Venkataraman (Venkatoo), so he was free and unattached. She sent one of Ramana's companions to Nagasundaram to tell him of her wish. In 1918 Nagasundaram left his job and came to Tiruvannamalai. First he lived at a friend's house and climbed up to the Ashram each day. Then he took a vow of renunciation and adopted the ochre robe of a *sannyasin*. His name was changed to Niranjanandaswami, but he was generally called 'Chinnaswami' (little Swami), because he was

---

[54] The Song of the Poppadam. In: Collected Works, p. 140

the brother of the big Swami. At first he used to go to town every day begging, later he gave it up as there was by now enough for all to eat in the Ashram itself.

The Ramana-family at Skandashram

Outwardly Sri Ramana seemed to have returned to a family life with regular household duties. According to the common view a householder is on a lower level than a *sadhu*, who no longer cares about worldly affairs. Once Seshadri Swami joked about this, saying to a man who wanted to visit the Maharshi, "Yes, go and see. There is a householder there. You will get sweet cakes there."

Alagammal's only desire was to be with Ramana at the moment of her death. When her daughter Alamelu invited her to the ceremony to open her new house, she declined, fearing that she would be unable to return to her son if she became sick there. She said to Ramana, "Even if you were to throw away my dead body in these thorny bushes I do not mind but I must end this life in your arms."

Since 1920 her health had been deteriorating. She was now unable to work very much and was forced to conserve her strength. Medication did not bring any improvement. During her sickness

Ramana spent a lot of time with her, he often spent the whole night seated at her bedside.

Mother's tiny room today

When Alagammal felt that her end was nearing, she called both her sons to her side, placed Chinnaswami's hand in the hand of Ramana and said to the latter one, "This boy does not know what is right and what is wrong. Don't let him go away from you. Keep a watchful eye on him. This is my last wish."

Chinnaswami stayed his whole life with his older brother. In 1929 he took over the Ashram management as *sarvadhikari*. Ramana always kept an eye on him and if there were any difficulties he found a tactful solution. For his part Chinnaswami was totally dedicated to his brother and had the greatest veneration for him.

On 19th May 1922 Alagammal's condition became critical. Kunju Swami reports, "After his morning walk, Sri Bhagavan went into mother's room and sat beside her. He ate his lunch there itself and was sitting beside her all the time. When he noticed her struggling for breath, he put his right hand on her chest. She became a little restful after a while. The time of mother's liberation was drawing near. Sri Bhagavan put one of his hands on her head and another on her chest and sat quietly."[55] The devotees had started to recite the *Vedas*, Akshara Mana Malai and the name of Ram simultaneously in three groups, to silence down her mind. At 8 p.m. Alagammal died. Ramana left his hands in this position on her chest and head until the last and also for a while after her death. Only then was he sure that she had attained liberation.

He had done the same at Palaniswami's death. The faithful attendant Palaniswami had continued living in the solitude of the Virupaksha Cave when Ramana moved to Skandashram. When Palaniswami became seriously ill, Maharshi visited him daily. At the hour of his death he also laid his right hand on the right side of his chest, the place of the spiritual heart (see also Chapter 18) and the left on his head. But with Palaniswami he had pulled away his hands too soon – as he reported himself, "In her case it was success; on a previous occasion I did the same for Palaniswami when the end was approaching, but it was a failure. He opened his eyes and passed away." At the last moment Palaniswami's mind and life force fled through the eyes instead of being absorbed in the heart centre.

When Sri Ramana came out of his mother's room his face shone with happiness about her liberation. There was no grief, because she had attained her goal. He said with relief, "Hereafter we can eat. Come on; there is no pollution."[56]

---

[55] Kunju Swami: Reminiscences, p. 62

[56] Death is seen to be a form of pollution and requires a purificatory rite for all those present in the house of the dead person. But if the deceased has attained liberation (*moksha*) and is no longer subject to rebirth, there is also no pollution. His/her mortal remains are not allowed to be cremated but must be buried. In Hinduism it is believed that the life breath and life stream of such a saint remain in such a body for thousands of years. Also his body requires no purification by fire. It is bathed, embalmed and placed into the grave in a seated position, with legs crossed.

Alagammal's face was shining and beaming like that of a yogi sunk in meditation. He himself described it in these words, "After mother breathed her last, her body glowed with a divine resplendence. Immediately after the body was bathed that effulgence subsided." When someone said that mother had passed away. Ramana corrected him saying, "No, she did not pass away, she was absorbed."

Mother's dead body was wrapped in a new sari and decorated with flowers, her forehead was signed with holy ashes (vibhuti). There were no purificatory rites. As she was liberated, her body was not to be burned. It was, however, decided to bury her near the Pali Teertham at the southern foot of Arunachala, as it was forbidden to perform cremations and burials on the hill. Throughout the night from 9 in the evening till 4 in the morning the *Tiruvasagam* of Manikkavasagar was recited. Arunachala Swami, Kunju Swami and Ramana recited it in turns. Some devotees went into town to obtain the preparations required for the burial ceremony. Early in the morning Ramana and his companions laid Alagammal on a stretcher made of bamboo and carried her down the hill. The cacti and the undergrowth had been cleared away from the place where she was to be buried.

In the meantime Alamelu had arrived along with her husband, her nephew Venkatoo and some devotees. Although it had been decided that Alagammal's burial should be a quiet affair, a huge crowd of Maharshi's devotees had come, bringing fruit, flowers and coconuts. A *Shiva lingam* was erected over the grave, which, at the suggestion of Ganapati Muni, was named Mathrubhutheswara (God in the form of the mother).

10. Ramanashram Comes into Being

Now you see what changes have come outwardly, what buildings have been raised and how the Ashram has grown all-round. But I am ever the Same.

The first building at Ramanashram

Puja was performed regularly each day at Alagammal's tomb (*samadhi*), ending at midday. As it was too hot to return to Skandashram a small hut was built which was used for cooking and the return journey to the Ashram was delayed until the evening. Eventually Chinnaswami decided to stay there permanently and lived in the hut along with Dandapaniswami. Due to the fact that some of the food now had to be brought here, there was at times not enough to eat in Skandashram. This led to differences of opinion, which Sri Ramana settled with his usual diplomacy.

Sri Ramana's followers soon noticed that he visited his mother's *samadhi* each day. They therefore started to wait for him there. One day he was invited to a lavish meal by a devotee. A large number of townspeople also turned up and the meal turned into a feast which continued into the evening. As nightfall had set in, Ramana was unable to return to Skandashram, so he remained at the foot of the hill overnight. The following day the same thing happened again. In addition, Ganapati Muni had joined them and gave an enthralling lecture which lasted late into the night. Over the days that followed Sri Ramana was always detained for some reason until it was too late to return to Skandashram.

Finally Kunju Swami and Gopal Rao were asked to look after Skandashram. For a week they waited for Ramana's return in vain. As they did not like to stay up there without their master they came back down and from that time on the Ashram was left empty. A short time later the deserted Ashram was broken into. Amongst other things the thieves removed a clock and a wooden plank which Ramana had used. When he heard about it, he said, "It is good. Nobody need go there to look after the place anymore."

This marked the beginning of Ramanashram. Sri Ramana once expressed it thus, "The same *shakti* (power) that had brought me from Madurai to Tiruvannamalai brought me down here from the hill."

In 1924 there was a robbery at the Ashram. One summer night Sri Ramana and four of his companions were sleeping in one of the thatched huts near the windows, when they heard thieves trying to climb in through the window. Kunju Swami was furious and wanted to confront the thieves, but Ramana dissuaded him saying, "Let these robbers play their role; we shall stick to ours. Let them do what they like; it is for us to bear and forebear. Let us not interfere with them." He suggested to the thieves that he and his companions would leave the hut so that they could take whatever they wanted. But when they came out, the robbers beat them with sticks. They also beat Ramana on his thigh, who said, "If you are not satisfied yet, you may strike the other leg also." And to Ramakrishna, who wanted to protect him, he said humorously, that he had only received his appropriate *puja* (*puja* in Tamil means worship but also beating).

The Ashram inmates waited in the northern hut while the thieves rummaged through everything. The things they found, however, were worth no more than a few rupees. Being extremely disappointed and not willing to believe that this was everything, one of them returned brandishing a stick and threatened, "Where is your money, where do you keep that?" Maharshi answered that there was no money as they were poor *sadhus* living upon alms.

At two in the morning the thieves finally left and Kunju Swami, who had managed to escape to get help from town, returned accompanied by several policemen. But Ramana was sitting in the northern hall conversing calmly with his disciples about spiritual matters as if nothing had happened.

In the early years Ramanashram consisted of just a few huts. The so-called Old Hall, in which Sri Ramana lived day and night until 1949, was built in 1928. It was here that the many meetings with visitors and devotees took place. The Old Hall, which measures 40 feet by 15, is not very spacious and contains only Ramana's sofa and some bookcases.

The story of the first couch is worth mentioning. Ramana used to sit on a simple wooden plank in a corner of the room. One day Rangaswami Gounder brought a couch as a gift for Ramana and asked him to sit on it. But Maharshi refused. For three days Gounder prayed that he may accept his present. On the third night Ramana finally gave way and laid down on the couch to sleep. From that moment on it became his place of residence day and night.

In 1925, in Palakothu on the western side of the Ashram, a colony came into being where *sadhus* and devotees lived in caves and in huts under the trees. This was the year in which B.V. Narasimha Swami[57], the first Ramana biographer, came to the Ashram. It was his intention to stay a long time, but as the Ashram resources were

---

[57] Narasimha Swami's Ramana biography "Self Realization" had already been published in 1931 and serves as a unique source for the early years of the Maharshi.

very limited, he decided to look after himself and built a small hut at Palakothu. He was soon joined by other devotees. As it had by now become the custom that only those who worked in the Ashram were allowed to stay there for any length of time, those who wanted to lead a meditative life built their huts in this colony and cared for themselves. Annamalai Swami lived there, when he was no longer working for the Ashram, also Kunju Swami, Yogi Ramiah, Muruganar, Paul Brunton, Viswanatha Swami, Ramanatha Brahmachari, Balarama Reddy and many others. Sri Ramana used to pass through the colony every day on his walks.

The Ashram grew steadily. Over the years, more buildings were erected, such as the store room, the office and the bookshop, the dispensary, the guest house for male visitors and a row of small bungalows for guests staying for longer periods. These were followed by the cowshed, the *Veda* school, the kitchen and the dining room. In 1937 the Ashram even opened its own post office.

Maharshi displayed a natural talent for planning building projects. Annamalai Swami gave detailed accounts of this in his reminiscences (Godman: Living by the Words of Bhagavan). For many years he was entrusted with the task of supervising the projects and received his instructions from Ramana directly. These instructions were never given in the form of a command but more in the form of a suggestion. So Ramana would say that he had just had this or that idea and that if he wanted to he could do it like that.

Sri Ramana inspected the work each day. Before work started he would explain to Annamalai Swami what needed to be done. Sometimes he would draw a few lines on a piece of paper to illustrate what he meant. Apart from these small sketches there were no construction drawings. All buildings originated from Ramana's simple plans, with the exception of the store room, which a local building contractor had drawn, and the Temple for the Mother, which was erected in accordance with the plans of a master temple builder. The engineers amongst the devotees offered their assistance in the form of construction drawings. All these plans were placed before Ramana, but without even unfolding them, he laid them aside and explained, "Before we came here all these buildings had already been planned by a higher power. At each destined moment all things will happen according to that plan. So why should we bother with all these written plans?"[58]

The impression which is sometimes given, that the Ashram came into being around the Maharshi without his participation, is therefore absolutely wrong, as Annamalai testified, "It was Bhagavan, and Bhagavan alone, who decided when buildings should be built, where they should be built, on what scale they should be constructed, what materials should be used, and who should be in charge of the construction."[59]

The financial side was the only aspect in which he did not interfere and which he left in full to Chinnaswami, who had taken over the Ashram management in 1929. Often there was no money available for new building projects, nevertheless Ramana initiated their start. Then Chinnaswami would complain about the imminent financial ruin the Ashram was facing, but sufficient donations were always received to enable the current project to be finished.

In 1942 the building of a small three-roomed hospital was started. It was designed to be used only for distributing medicine to out-patients and as a first aid station, but it was here that the operations were later carried out to treat Sri Ramana's cancers. Sri Ramana showed particular interest in the construction of this building. Annamalai Swami, who once again was entrusted with managing the project, reports, "When there was little or no work going on, and nothing of interest to inspect, he would still come to the site and sit there for long periods. On these occasions he would often look at me and give me the same type of *darshan*, involving a direct transmission of grace through the eyes, that he frequently gave to devotees in the Hall."[60]

---

[58] Godman: Living by the Words, p. 163
[59] dto., p. 161
[60] dto., p. 207

Ramanashram in later years

Sri Ramana not only took great interest in the various building works, gave advice and instructions and each evening asked for a progress report from Annamalai Swami, he also liked to participate in the work himself. He evidently felt more comfortable on the building site outside, than on his couch. He would have liked to have participated more fully in this physical work, if only his devotees had allowed him. But they thought it inappropriate for him to do strenuous physical labour. In addition, he also had to care for the increasing numbers of visitors, who often came from afar for the sole purpose of having his *darshan*. Once when he was visiting the building site, his attendant Madhava Swami announced the arrival of new visitors, Sri Ramana replied jokingly that a new warrant had been issued for his arrest and it was now time for him to return to jail.

One of the most important and lengthy building projects was the erection of the new temple over the mother's *samadhi*. The project was started on 1st September 1939, exactly 43 years after Sri Ramana's arrival at Tiruvannamalai. Again he showed great interest in the construction work. Exceptionally it was not he who did the drawings but a master temple builder, who brought with him several stonemasons experienced in temple construction.

The temple building placed an enormous strain on the Ashram finances. Chinnaswami obtained the best teak wood from Burma and wanted to use only the highest quality material. At times there was not enough money to pay the workers, but then, unexpectedly, donations would be received.

Feroza Taleyarkhan[61], a member of an aristocratic Parsi family, reports how she raised considerable funds for the mother's temple and the New Hall on behalf of Chinnaswami. Ramana, however, was insistent that the collections should not be done in his name.

The construction of the temple took nearly 10 years. It was called Mathrubhuteswara (God in the form of the mother) and was ceremonially opened in March 1949. The official ceremony (*kumbhabhishekam*) lasted for four days. On the last evening but one before the feast, the *Sri Chakra Meru* was installed in the inner shrine. Major Chadwick reports how Ramana himself supervised the installation, "It was an extremely hot night and with three charcoal retorts for melting the cement adding to the heat, it must have been intolerable inside the airless cave of the inner shrine, but for about an hour and a half Bhagavan sat there telling the workmen what to do. On the last night of the function he went in procession, opening the doors of the New Hall and temple and passing straight up into the Inner Shrine, where he stood for some five minutes with both hands laid on the *Sri Chakra* in blessing."[62]

At the time of the *kumbhabhishekam* Sri Ramana was ill with cancer and had already been operated upon twice. The New Hall was finished at the same time as the mother's temple. The Old Hall had become far too small to accommodate the large numbers of visitors.

---

[61] Feroza Taleyarkhan also played an important role in the renovation of the Patala Lingam and in the purchase of Ramana's birth house in Tiruchuli (Sundaram Mandiram) and the house in Madurai (Ramana Mandiram) through Ramanashram.
[62] Chadwick: Reminiscences, pp. 59ff

These were the last buildings to be constructed during the Maharshi's lifetime.

11. Sri Ramana in the Kitchen

You must cover your vegetables when you cook them. Then only will they keep their flavour and be fit for food. It is the same with the mind. You must put a lid over it and let it simmer quietly. Then only does a man become food fit for God to eat.

In the early years at Ramanashram the food was quite simple, it was only in later years that there were large numbers of visitors, so it did not take long to cook the meals. In Ramana's words, "A big vessel used to be put on the fire. Whatever vegetables were received till noon used to be cut and put into it, boiled and *sambar* made. There was no ladle even to stir and mix them. We used to take a piece of firewood, chisel it and use it for stirring those vegetables in the vessel. That preparation was the only side dish. When we mixed it with rice and ate, it used to be very tasty. The labour also was comparatively less."[63]

As the Ashram grew and the number of visitors increased, the cooking also became more complicated and time-consuming. Up until the late 1920s Chinnaswami acted as the main cook, with the assistance of Dandapani Swami and others. When he became the Ashram manager, he was replaced in the kitchen by a number of Brahmin widows - Santammal, Lokammal, Subbalakshmi Ammal, Sampurnamma and others. Only members of the Brahmin caste were allowed to do the cooking. This orthodox caste rule was observed because of the Brahmins, as otherwise they would have eaten nothing from the Ashram kitchen.

But, for a long time, overall supervision was the responsibility of Sri Ramana himself. He was the first to appear in the kitchen, long before sunrise, preparing breakfast and helping at times to cook lunch or giving instructions on how it was to be prepared. Sampurnamma remembers, "In the evening, before I would leave the Ashram for the town to sleep, he would ask me what there was

---

[63] Nagamma: Letters, p. 388

to be cooked the next day. Then, arriving at day-break the next morning, I would find everything ready – vegetables peeled and cut, lentils soaked, spices ground, coconut scraped. As soon as he saw me in the kitchen, he would give detailed instructions about what should be cooked and how. He would then sit in the Hall awhile and then return to the kitchen to see how things were moving, taste them now and then, and go back to the Hall, to come again an hour or two later."[64]

This way Ramana remained in constant contact with the kitchen, even while he was seated in the Hall.

G.V. Subbaramayya, a college professor and poet, used to visit the Ashram regularly during his college vacation. Whilst staying there from April to June 1940 he helped Sri Ramana with the preparation of breakfast in the kitchen. "The hours of duty were between 2.30 a.m. and 4 a.m. Sri Bhagavan would come punctually at 2.30 a.m. and first spend some time in cutting vegetables with the workers and devotees. Then He would enter the kitchen and prepare *sambar* or chutney for breakfast, and occasionally some extra dishes also. ... At first I was an ignoramus in the work. ... I did not know at first how to hold the pestle and grind. Sri Bhagavan placed His hand upon mine and turned the pestle in the proper way. Again what a thrill! ... After the work was finished, Sri Bhagavan would take out a bit from the dish, taste a little of it and give us the remainder to taste, and sometimes when our hands were unwashed, He would Himself throw it into our mouths with His own hand. That would be the climax of our happiness. Then He would hasten back to the Hall and lie reclining on the couch and appear dozing as the Brahmins arrived for *parayana* [singing of the *Vedas*]." [65]

Work with Sri Ramana had both its difficult moments and its pleasant moments. Although he was full of kindness he was also a strict disciplinarian and would not tolerate the slightest negligence. Everything had to be done perfectly and with full awareness. He demanded that his instructions be followed to the letter.

---

[64] Sampurnamma: Bhagavan in the Kitchen. In: Ramana Smrti, p. [132]
[65] Subbaramayya: Reminiscences, pp. 70ff

One evening a disciple who was a solicitor, insisted on helping with the work. He was asked to move a vessel containing *sambar*. As he moved it some drops spilled over the sides. At once Bhagavan said, "You are fit only for arguing before the Court. This work is not for you."

Kunju Swami narrates, "Sri Bhagavan used to go into the kitchen by 4 a.m. and start cutting vegetables; one or two of us would also join and help. Sometimes the amount of vegetables used to startle us. Bhagavan managed to cut much more and more quickly than the rest of us. At such times we would look up at the clock in our impatience to finish the job and try and have another nap. Bhagavan would sense our impatience and say: 'Why do you look at the clock?' We tried to bluff Bhagavan saying: 'If only we could complete the work before 5, we could meditate for an hour.' Bhagavan would mildly retort: 'The allotted work has to be completed in time. Other thoughts are obstacles, not the amount of work. Doing the allotted work in time is itself meditation. Go ahead and do the job with full attention.'"[66]

Sri Ramana was a perfect cook. He never added too much or too little salt or spices. Sampurnamma reports, "As long as we followed his instructions, everything would go well with our cooking. But the moment we would act on our own we would be in trouble. Even then, if we sought his help, he would taste our brew and tell us what to do and what to add to make the food good for serving. We thus came to know fully that in dealing with him our only duty was to obey. This training became a part of our lives. By daily practice we learned to have our minds always focussed on Bhagavan. Whenever we were afraid, anxious or in pain, we had only to think of him and we felt his helping hand."[67]

The Ashram did not have the means to increase the number of staff, so there was always plenty of work to do in the kitchen. An unwritten rule demanded that the kitchen helpers had to continue

---

[66] Ganesan: Moments, pp. 107ff
[67] Sampurnamma: Bhagavan in the Kitchen. In: Ramana Smrti, pp. [132ff]

working until the last meal had been served and cleared away. Chinnaswami did not allow any of them to stay in the Hall to meditate or to listen to the talks when they were supposed to be working. Sundaram reports, "When we would sneak in and hide ourselves behind people's backs, Bhagavan would look at us significantly, as if saying, 'Better go to your work. Don't ask for trouble.'"

When the cook Subbalakshmi Ammal wanted to meditate more and complained that the kitchen work would take up all of her time, Ramana answered, "If you identify yourself with the body, you are bound to dualities. Work would appear difficult. Even if we free ourselves from work will the mind cease to wander? It does not let us even sleep in peace. It keeps wandering as in dreams." [68]

But in the evening, after the visitors had left, the kitchen workers had Ramana to themselves. He then chatted with them, made them laugh, asked about their health and gave instructions for the following day.

Everybody knew that Sri Ramana was very careful with everything, particularly with food, and never wasted anything. This was, of course, especially noticeable in the kitchen. When once some mustard seeds fell on the floor, the cooks took no notice, but Ramana picked them up one by one with his fingernails and placed them in a small bowl. Raja Iyer reports that Ramana had shown him how to use the ladle in such a way as to avoid a single morsel of food falling on the floor, how to pour without spilling anything and how to make a fire with only a few drops of kerosene.

For each vegetable Ramana knew a special kind of preparation. Nothing was thrown away. If he cut spinach, he separated the leaves, the stalks and the roots. With the leaves he made the curry, the stalks were bound together, cooked and put into the *sambar* and the roots were washed carefully, squeezed and their juice put into

---

[68] Unforgettable Years, p. 87

the *rasam*. Any orange peel or apple peel was put into the chutney. The leftovers from the previous day were warmed up and served at the following breakfast, along with the *iddlies*. If there was any soup or vegetables left, they were put into the *sambar*. This was against the caste rules of the Brahmins, according to which leftovers may not be used the following day. But Ramana insisted that the avoidance of waste was more important than anything else. To give the leftovers to beggars was also not practicable, as they had to have the same as everyone else and not be given poor quality food.

One evening Ramana had cut spinach and *brinjal* (aubergines) and laid aside the pieces which he could not use so as to make use of them the following day. The next morning, when he came into the kitchen as usual and asked for the pieces he had put aside, he was told that they had already been thrown away. He therefore went outside, found them, cleaned them, cut them into smaller pieces and used them.

Sampurnamma recounted another story along the same lines, "Once a feast was being prepared for his birthday. Devotees sent food in large quantities: some sent rice, some sugar, some fruits. Someone sent a huge load of *brinjals* and we ate *brinjals* day after day. The stalks alone made a big heap which was lying in a corner. Bhagavan asked us to cook them as a curry! I was stunned, for even cattle would refuse to eat such useless stalks. Bhagavan insisted that the stalks were edible, and we put them in a pot to boil along with dry peas. After six hours of boiling they were as hard as ever. We were at a loss what to do, yet we did not dare to disturb Bhagavan. But he always knew when he was needed in the kitchen and he would leave the Hall even in the middle of a discussion. A casual visitor would think that his mind was all on cooking. … 'How is the curry getting on?' he asked. 'Is it a curry we are cooking? We are boiling steel nails!' I exclaimed, laughing. He stirred the stalks with the ladle and went away without saying anything. Soon after we found them quite tender. The dish was simply delicious and everybody was asking for a second helping. Bhagavan challenged the diners to guess what vegetable they were eating. Everybody praised the curry and the cook, except Bhagavan. He swallowed the little he was served in one mouth-full like a medicine and refused a second helping. I was very disappointed, for I had taken so much trouble to cook his stalks and he would not even taste them properly.

The next day he was telling somebody, 'Sampurnam was distressed that I did not eat her wonderful curry. Can she not see that everyone who eats is myself? And what does it matter who eats the food? It is the cooking that matters, not the cook or the eater. A thing done well, with love and devotion, is its own reward. What happens to it later matters little, for it is out of our hands."[69]

One of Sri Ramana's particularities should be mentioned at this point. Since his enlightenment experience in Madurai, what he ate meant nothing to him. He no longer had any preferences. This was evident in his later eating habits, as he liked to mix the various sour, sweet and spicy dishes together into a mash on his banana leaf. When once a lady devotee served him a variety of dishes, he asked her not to take so much trouble in future on his account, saying, "All of you have many tastes but I have only one taste; your taste is in the many, mine is in the one." Then he mixed it all together to a mash and ate it.

On another occasion he said, "What is taste? It is what our tongue tells us. We think that taste is in the food itself, but it is not so. The food itself is neither tasty nor not tasty; it is the tongue that makes it so. To me no taste is pleasant or unpleasant, it is just as it is."[70]

Although Sri Ramana was an excellent cook, took great care in the preparation of the meals and did not tolerate any carelessness on the part of the cooks, the pleasure of eating seemed to mean nothing to him.

At the end of the 1930s he stopped cooking, as the stream of visitors was growing ever larger and building projects increasingly

---

[69] Sampurnamma: Bhagavan in the Kitchen. In: Ramana Smrti, p. [132]
[70] Lokammal: Sri Ramanasramam. In: Ramana Smrti, p. [101]

demanded his attention. But even so he still remained in constant contact with the kitchen.

12. Daily Life at the Ashram

Let activities go on. They do not affect the pure Self. The difficulty is that people think they are the doer. This is a mistake. It is the higher power which does everything and people are only tools. If they accept that position they will be free from troubles, otherwise they court them.

Ordered Daily Routine

Life at the Ashram was extremely well-ordered. Tidiness, cleanliness, thrift and punctuality were expected from everyone. Arthur Osborne remarked, "Bhagavan Sri Ramana was meticulously exact, closely observant, practical and humorous. His daily life was conducted with a punctiliousness that Indians today would have to call pure Western. In everything he was precise and orderly. The Ashram Hall was swept out several times daily. The books were always in their places. The cloths covering the couch were scrupulously clean and beautifully folded. The loin-cloth, which was all he wore, was gleaming white. The two clocks in the Hall were adjusted daily to radio time. The calendar was never allowed to fall behind the date. The routine of life flowed to a regular pattern."[71]

In the later years, when Ramana had ceased working in the kitchen and had started to supervise the building projects, his timetable was as follows - he would rise at approximately 3.30 a.m., at half past five he took his bath and at half past six breakfast was served. This was followed by the first walk on the hill. At 8.30 he read the incoming mail and at 9.45 he made a short visit to the cowshed. Lunch was served at 11.30. Around midday he went for a second walk, which this time lasted an hour and took him to Palakothu. At 2.30 p.m. there was coffee and at approximately 4 p.m. he read the outgoing mail. Half an hour later he again went for a walk for an hour. After this the *Veda parayana* was chanted, followed by the

---

[71] Lokammal: Sri Ramanasramam. In: Ramana Smrti, p. [101]

Tamil *parayana*. At half past seven the bell called everyone to dinner. Afterwards Ramana went to the cowshed again and at 8.45 p.m. all devotees retired to their lodgings.

Ramana in the Old Hall

It is reported that Sri Ramana slept very little at night. He also never lay down flat, but remained upright, leaning against the back of the couch. After lunch everyone in the Ashram liked to withdraw to take a nap – not so Ramana. He often made use of this quiet hour to feed the animals or make a round through the Ashram and inform himself of the progress of the building projects.

In spite of the increasing numbers of visitors Sri Ramana led an active life. In addition to cooking and supervising the building projects, he read the proofs of the books which were to be published. By now his works had been translated and printed in a number of Indian dialects. He had written his famous hymns to Arunachala around 1914. From 1923 to 1929 he wrote Upadesa Saram (The Essence of Instruction in 30 Verses), Upadesa Manjari (Spiritual

Instruction) and Ulladu Narpadu (Reality in Forty Verses) with supplementary verses. This was followed in the thirties and forties by various translations into Tamil, Malayam and Telugu of important *advaita* scriptures, such as certain parts of *Vivekachudamani* and other scriptures by *Shankara*, some verses of the *Bhagavad Gita* and parts of the *Agamas*. The English translations of all these works can be found in 'The Collected Works of Ramana Maharshi'. So Ramana regularly spent a lot of time proof-reading these publications. He also read everything that was written about him and was very particular that everything should be accurate. When a biography was to be published about him in Telugu, entitled 'Ramana Leela', he painstakingly went through it correcting any mistakes.

He was equally conscientious in the way he dealt with the incoming and outgoing mail. He read all the incoming letters and although he never answered letters himself, others did this for him, he carefully read through the outgoing mail and made corrections if need be or gave instructions as to how the answer should be phrased.

He also did bookbinding work. Now and then people would bring him old books in poor condition. He checked whether they were complete, added any missing pages by copying them out himself and inserting them, and then repaired the books.

Just as he never wasted any food, so he also never wasted any paper. He would collect any paper which was still usable, often cutting it up into small sheets, which he would then bind together to make notebooks. Even the pins from the newspapers would be kept. "They will otherwise be merely thrown away. We shall use them. How should we get new ones? They have to be bought. Where is the money?", he would say.

The regular walks were also a fixed part of the daily routine, though they became shorter as the numbers of visitors increased and the various building projects were commenced. In the later years especially, he was not able to put a foot outside the door without being accompanied by a small crowd of people. Solitary walks on the hill had become impossible, although at times he managed to slip away without letting anyone know, as soon as people noticed, they all wanted to come with him. As happened one day when he wanted to go up to Skandashram alone. The result was a kind of mass migration. When he was asked by his devotees to climb to the top of the hill with them, as he knew the way best, he replied jokingly, "If I come, everyone in the Ashram will join me. Even the buildings will come with us!"

In the later years the restrictions became so great that he could no longer move around freely. Everything was governed by a timetable. A barrier was erected to prevent people touching him. He called this enclosure his 'cage'. "They have put bars around me, though wooden, as in the gaol. I may not cross these bars. There are people specially deputed to watch me and they keep watch on me by turns. I can't move about as I like; they are there to prevent it. One person goes and another comes according to turns. What is the difference between these people and the police except that the former are not in uniform? ... Even if I want to go out to answer calls of nature, they must follow me to protect me. Even my going out must be according to the scheduled time."[72]

In the early years Sri Ramana attempted on a couple of occasions to leave the Ashram for a life of solitude. Vasudeva (the same who once witnessed Ramana's second death experience at Tortoise rock) relates, "Once Bhagavan and I went round the hill during the Skandashram days. When we reached near Esanya *math* about 8.30 a.m., Bhagavan sat on a rock and said with tears in his eyes he would never again come to the Ashram and would go where he pleased and live in the forests or caves away from all men. I would not leave him and he would not come. It became very late. We went there about 8 or 8.30 a.m. and even when it became 1 p.m. we were still in this deadlock. Bhagavan asked me to go into the town and eat

---

[72] Nagamma: Letters, p. 366

my food and then come back if I wanted. But I was afraid that if I went Bhagavan would go away somewhere."[73]

Finally the Swami of Esanya *math* passed and invited Ramana to the *math*. With that the escape attempt was failed and he had no other choice than to return to Skandashram with Vasudeva.

Sri Ramana also reports about two other escape attempts, "Another time too I wanted to run away from all this crowd and live somewhere unknown, freely as I liked. That was when I was in Virupaksha Cave. ... But on that occasion my plans were frustrated by Yogananda Swami. I tried to be free on a third occasion also. That was after mother's passing away. I did not want to have even an Ashram like Skandashram and the people that were coming there then. But the result has been this Ashram [Ramanashram] and all the crowd here. Thus all my three attempts failed."[74]

When someone remarked that Sri Ramana could leave the Ashram when he liked, he replied, "What can I do? If I go off to the forest and try to hide, what will happen? They will soon find me out. Then someone will put up a hut in front of me and another person at the back, and it will not be long before huts will have sprung up on either side. Where can I go? I shall always be a prisoner."[75]

Another fixed part of the daily schedule was the chanting of the *Veda parayana*. At first, Brahmin boys used to come from town to do the chanting. Later, with the assistance of Major Chadwick, the Ashram opened its own *Veda* school (patasala), which is still in existence today.

The chanting of the *Vedas* in the morning and evening lasted around 40 minutes. Texts from the *Vedas* were recited, as well as other Sanskrit texts, such as for example the Forty Verses in Praise of Ramana by Ganapati Muni and Sri Ramana's Arunachala

---

[73] Mudaliar: Day by Day, pp. 275ff
[74] dto., p. 276
[75] Sadhu Arunachala: Reminiscences, p. 93

Pancharatna and Upadesa Saram. This was then followed by the so-called Tamil *Parayana* with other works by Sri Ramana.

Strictly speaking only Brahmins are allowed to be present at the *Veda Parayana*, but Sri Ramana wanted everyone to participate, so Brahmins sat next to non-Brahmins and Indians next to Westerners.

The Maharshi attached great importance to this chanting, stressing its calming effect upon the mind. If he was asked if people should not also understand the texts, he would say that it was not necessary, it was sufficient to use them as an aid to meditation. He himself would sit upright on his couch during the chanting, his eyes taking on a faraway look.

The Ashram Management

The various Ashram rules had to be followed by all. For example it was considered important that men and women should sit in separate areas in the Hall. Women were not allowed to stay in the Ashram overnight. In general only those who worked in the Ashram were allowed to live there. Anyone who wanted to meditate could take up residence at the Palakothu *sadhu* colony, but they had to take care of themselves. Families lived in Ramana Nagar, a settlement near the Ashram. The rich devotee Gounder (the same one who had offered the first couch to Sri Ramana) had purchased the area for this purpose. So in the Ashram itself there was only accommodation for visitors and devotees who worked there, with one or two exceptions, such as, for example, Major Chadwick, Devaraja Mudaliar and Yogi Ramiah.

Sri Ramana left the management of the Ashram to his brother. As *sarvadhikari*, Chinnaswami endeavoured to retain full control over everything that happened there. This frequently led to arguments with devotees who disagreed with his decisions. But whatever was eventually decided had to be accepted by all. If someone complained to Sri Ramana about Chinnaswami, the Maharshi protected his brother and never reversed his decisions.

If a devotee was guilty of a serious breach of the management rules, he could be banned from entering the Ashram, but this was generally only a temporary exclusion. It was enough to apologize or to promise to abide by the rules in future, to be allowed to return.

There was no point in complaining to Sri Ramana, as he never interfered in such disputes. When Ganapati Sastri (not to be confused with Ganapati Muni) was banished from the Ashram, he complained to Sri Ramana, "Chinnaswami has told me not to come to the Ashram. Bhagavan is just sitting like a stone Vinayaka statue. I have served the Ashram for a long time. I have also donated three almiras [cupboards] full of books to the Ashram. Will Bhagavan not ask Chinnaswami why he is not allowing me to come to the Ashram?"[76] But he received no answer to his complaint.

Whenever someone wanted to interfere in Ashram affairs Ramana would warn, "People walk up the drive to the Ashram in search of deliverance and then get caught up in Ashram politics and forget what they came for. If such matters were their concern they need not have come to Tiruvannamalai for them."[77] And to enthusiastic reformers he advised that it would be sufficient for them to reform themselves.

If conflicts were brought to him to settle he would answer, "If people with different opinions give up their *mouna* (silence) which is the embodiment of love, and come to me and say, 'We will do this,' and 'We will do that,' and enquire of me what I like better of the two, what can I say? If you all agree upon a course of action and then ask me for my opinion, I would then say it is all right. But when you are of two opinions, why do you come to me and ask me which I like the better? What I like is, to know who I am and to remain as I am with the knowledge that what is to happen will

---

[76] Godman: Living by the Words, p. 199
[77] Osborne: Ramana Maharshi and the Path, p. 120

happen and what is not to happen will not happen. Is that not right? Do you now understand what Bhagavan likes best?"[78]

There were, however, cases when Maharshi raised objections. When, for example, the Ashram management decided to close the doors of the Hall for two hours after lunch because of his weakened health, he protested by leaving the Hall and sitting outside to welcome the visitors, commenting, "The management is welcome to close the doors but I am free to meet the visitors here." In cases such as this, where the decision of the management meant that his devotees were prevented from coming to him for a time or if it would lead to some injustice, he could be uncompromising, saying, "You can look after your Ashram. I am going back to the hill."

Sri Ramana's Personal Attendants

Sri Ramana's personal attendants were chosen by Chinnaswami. Ramana himself never asked anyone to serve him, nor ever sent away an attendant who had been allotted to him. It became the tradition in the Ashram that the attendants were always young unmarried men. Annamalai Swami reports, "Once, when a woman who was a qualified nurse from North India volunteered to be an attendant, Bhagavan replied by saying, 'Ask the people in the Hall'. Krishnaswami, the chief attendant, and some of the other people in the Hall objected. 'No! No! We cannot have ladies doing service to Bhagavan. It is not proper.' Bhagavan turned to the woman and said, 'These people all think like this. What can I do?'"[79]

One of the attendants' tasks was to receive the food offerings brought by devotees and give some of it back to them as *prasadam*. They had to be careful that the men sat on one side of the Hall and the women on the other. Whenever Maharshi left the Hall, one of them had to accompany him. The other one stayed back to clean the Hall. The cloths on the couch had to be kept clean. Washing the

---

[78] Nagamma: Letters, p. 385
[79] Godman: Living by the Words, p. 96

cloths and preparing warm water for the morning bath was also the duty of the attendants, as was accompanying Ramana on his nightly walks to the toilet. There was, therefore, someone there to be helpful to him round the clock.

Ramana with attendant on the hill

Sri Ramana was strict with his attendants, insisting that they carry out their duties meticulously and punctually. He did not let them get away with anything.

At first, Krishnaswami often used to fail to chase away the monkeys during their raids into the Hall to steal fruit. He was rebuked for this by Sri Ramana. Thereafter Krishnaswami became a keen monkey chaser. He armed himself with a catapult and drove the monkeys away with it as soon as they appeared.

Something similar happened with the attendant Rangaswami, who also failed to chase away the monkeys and instead liked to meditate. Ramana scolded him, "If you want to meditate like this, go somewhere else. If you want to live here you must do service like everyone else. Meditation is contained in your service to the Guru."[80]

One of Sri Ramana's characteristics was that he never asked for anything. If the attendant had no idea of what he might need he did not ask for it. He did not want anyone to be troubled on his behalf, not even his attendants. So the attendants were trained to know what Sri Ramana might want, whether it be something to drink, to wash his hands or to read the newspaper – they knew without him having to say. They were helped by the fact that there was a fixed time for almost everything.

Major Chadwick tells the story of the *betel*. In this case the attendant's omission resulted in Ramana simply giving up chewing *betel*. "One morning Bhagavan was about to go out and was only waiting for the attendant to give him the *betel*, which was always placed by his side when it was time for his walk. For some reason the attendant did not do it, everybody in the Hall was waiting expectantly but could do nothing about it as the management did not allow anybody to attend on Bhagavan except those who had been specially detailed. Eventually Bhagavan got up and left the Hall without it. From that day on he never chewed again."[81]

Although Sri Ramana could be very strict with his attendants, he was also very concerned for their welfare. In summer, when he used to walk to Palakothu between midday and 1.30 p.m., the sandy path was so hot that walking barefoot could be very painful. Ramana always walked at the same steady pace, whether it was raining cats and dogs or whether the sun was blazing down, but he used to say to the attendant walking behind him, "Run, run and take shelter under that tree. Put your upper cloth under your feet and stand on it for a while."

---

[80] dto., p. 97
[81] Sadhu Arunachala: Reminiscences, p. 36

Similarly Ramana's concern was extended to Rangaswami, when he had to copy out several pages of a book. "One day Bhagavan asked me if I had completed the job. 'I do not have the time for it', I said. 'What are you doing now?' he queried. 'I am going to Palakothu to wash your cod-piece'. Bhagavan said, 'Okay, you do my job and I will do yours', so saying, he copied the remaining pages."[82]

Meals in the Ashram

In the dining hall today

Sri Ramana always took care that devotees had enough to eat. Often he personally ensured that they were served a meal upon their arrival at the Ashram.

One of Sri Ramana's principles was that under no circumstances did he want to be treated differently or better than anyone else. This was particularly apparent in the dining hall. In order to be sure that all

---

[82] Unforgettable Years, p. 53

were served the same as he himself, he took very little if he was served first. He later insisted that all others had to be served first and that he should be served last. One day when Suri Nagamma was handing out fruit from her nephew in the Hall, she served Sri Ramana first, then everybody else. At the end it was found that there was not enough fruit for everyone. So one of the attendants cut the remaining bananas into small pieces. Ramana said indignantly, "This is what I don't like. Why do you serve when you cannot give the same quantity to all people? ...

If you serve Bhagavan after you serve all the others, there will be equal distribution. If by chance nothing remains, it does not matter if I don't get anything; if all eat, I am satisfied even if I do not get my share."[83]

To prevent those sitting in the last rows being at a disadvantage and having nothing of the best dishes left for them, he would wait until the very last person had been served before eating. It was his general custom not to touch anything on his banana leaf until all had the same on theirs as he himself.

On special occasions such as his birthday (*jayanti*), the anniversary of his mother's death (*mahapuja*) and at *Kartikai Deepam*, lots of people, often hundreds and in the later years even thousands, came, all of whom had to be fed. On such days meals had to be served in several shifts. Ramana then liked to join the last group.

The principle of equality of all was also respected with regard to the daily feeding of the poor, which took place at 11 a.m., whereas devotees and Ramana had their lunch at 11.30 only. The poor received the same food as the Ashram inhabitants. He was very particular about this too. One day he noticed that the feeding of the poor outside was not carried out correctly and one of them did not receive his share. The next day, when the poor had formed a queue for their meal, he went outside and said to those serving, "If you do

---

[83] Nagamma: Letters, pp. 291ff

not give them food first, I will not come to the dining hall at all. I will stand under the tree along with these people, stretch out my hands for food like them, and when I am given a ball of food, I will eat it, go straight to the Hall and sit there."[84]

There are lots of dining hall stories which make clear how fiercely Maharshi resisted any preferential treatment of his person, as, again and again, devotees tried to serve him a special delicacy or a larger share than others. The cook Santamma also had to learn her lesson. At the beginning of her stay at the Ashram she served Sri Ramana an extra portion on his leaf, which he at once noticed saying angrily, "Why did you serve the Swami more of the curry than the rest? Have you come all the way here to learn this? If you serve more to others and less to me I would be happy. Do you want to purchase grace by serving extra? If you show the devotees the same love as you have for me, then your love for me too will grow."[85]

Sri Ramana did not want anything special done for his health. Once he alone was served rice whereas everyone else was served boiled wheat. When he asked Chinnaswami why this was, he was told, "Wheat is not good for Sri Bhagavan's health." Ramana retorted, "Oho! Are you a doctor? Serve me the same as is served to others. Make no discrimination." And when someone suggested that Ramana should regularly take orange juice for his health, he said, that in that case 200 glasses of juice would be needed. "Do you want me alone to gulp down the drink with all of you watching, empty-handed? Moreover, how can poor people like us provide for 200 tumblers of juice, paying Rs 50 every day."

Mudaliar Patti, also known as Mudaliar Granny, and Echammal, who had both been bringing food up the hill to Sri Ramana since the early years, refused to be deprived of this privilege in later years. They used to cook at home and bring the lunch to the Ashram in a basket. Echammal cooked enough for around two people, Mudaliar Patti for four. Both had the privilege of serving their food personally

---

[84] dto., p. 427
[85] Unforgettable Years, p. 73

to Ramana and the devotees. When the kitchen at Ramanashram was better equipped this no longer made any sense. Ramana asked the women to spare themselves the trouble in future, but they were so fond of it that he didn't insist.

For the Brahmins' sakes a certain importance was attached to the observation of caste rules. Brahmins are only allowed to eat together with members of their own caste. To enable them to obey this rule the dining hall was separated in two by a bamboo screen. On the one side the Brahmins had their place, on the other side the non-Brahmins. Sri Ramana sat in the opening of the screen on the non-Brahmin side and was visible to all. Again and again Brahmins tried to sit on the non-Brahmin side and circumvent their own caste rules in the Ashram. They argued that with Ramana there were no caste differences. But he did not accept their arguments as long as they continued to apply caste rules at home.

Apart from this, no differences were made in the dining hall and in the Hall. The poor sat alongside the rich, the educated alongside simple workers.

Festivals at the Ashram

There was always a great celebration for Sri Ramana's birthday (*jayanti*), which, according to the Tamil calendar, falls either at the end of December or at the beginning of January. The custom was started in 1912, when he was living in the Virupaksha Cave and when, for the first time, devotees organized a feast for him. At first he refused and wrote down the following two verses, explaining his reasons, "You who wish to celebrate a birthday, inquire first who was born. One's true birthday is when one enters into the Eternal Being which shines for ever without birth or death. Of all days on one's birthday one should mourn one's fall (into *samsara*). To celebrate it as a festival is like adorning and glorifying a corpse. To seek one's Self and merge in it is wisdom."[86]

A celebration at the Ashram

But Ramana's protests were to no avail. His followers argued that they were celebrating his birthday for their own sakes and Maharshi need have nothing to worry about. So the festival became a tradition. Sri Ramana sat outside on his couch or on a podium decorated with flowers. Music was played, poems were read in different languages to honour him and a festival meal was served. Any poor person who came to the Ashram received a meal. In the later years the festival was attended by thousands with the police and Scouts being deployed to ensure that everything ran smoothly.

The anniversary of Alagammal's burial (*mahapuja*) and *Kartikai Deepam* were celebrated in the same way as *jayanti*. Major Chadwick writes in his reminiscences, "Bhagavan always radiated tremendous peace, but on those occasions when crowds were

---

[86] Collected Works, p. 143

attracted to the Ashram such as *jayanti, mahapuja, Deepam* and such functions, this increased to an extraordinary degree."[87]

---

[87] Sadhu Arunachala: Reminiscences, p. 36

13. Sri Ramana and His Devotees

Muruganar, "I was confident that even the mere Presence of this great Sadguru would do everything for me."

Muruganar

The Tamil Poet Muruganar came to Sri Ramana in 1923. He was one of the devotees who was especially close to him. He was named 'Bhagavan's shadow', as he was so dedicated to Ramana that he followed him everywhere. Even before he saw the Maharshi for the first time Muruganar knew that in him he had found his guru.

As he was a poet he presented his new master with a poem, in which he praised him as 'Guru Ramana Shiva'. When Muruganar arrived, Ramana was just coming out of the Hall to start his walk on the hill. Muruganar stood rooted to the spot. Sri Ramana glanced at him and then asked him to read the poem he had brought. Muruganar tried to read, but was so moved that he started to cry and lost his voice. "Can't you read it? Then I will read it myself", said Maharshi and he read out the poem. As Muruganar reports, he lost his individual ego that very day and became 'Bhagavan's shadow'.

Once he said about Sri Ramana, "He is the robber chief. He has taken three – my body, my mind and life itself – and given in return one only, that One, Indivisible Supreme!"

From his first meeting with the Maharshi until his death in 1973 Muruganar wrote many thousands of verses in Tamil, which were exclusively devoted to the teaching of his master and his praise. He also had an important role to play in the origin of Sri Ramana's works Ulladu Narpadu, Atma Vidya and Upadesa Saram.

Devotees and Visitors

It was in the thirties that the fame of Sri Ramana started to spread throughout the world. In 1931 Narasimha Swami published the first English Ramana biography 'Self Realization'. Some years later Paul Brunton's book 'A Search in Secret India' was published in England. It became a best-seller and introduced Sri Ramana to the West.

Over the next few years many new devotees came to join him. Some of them stayed with him their whole lives, for example the Englishman Major Chadwick (Sadhu Arunachala), Balarama Reddy and many others. In 1932, M.A. Piggot was the first Western woman to visit him. More Westerners followed, such as Maurice Frydman and the famous film star Mercedes De Acosta. In 1938 Mercedes De Acosta spoke with Sri Ramana about the spiritual Heart. He pointed to the right side of her chest and said, "Here lies the Heart". This made such a deep impression on her that she gave her autobiography the title 'Here lies the Heart'. Paramahansa Yogananda and Swami Ramdas were also among the visitors. A meeting with Mahatma Gandhi almost took place, when one day Gandhi gave a talk in Tiruvannamalai. But as his car drove past the Ashram gate, his companion gave a sign to the driver to drive on and so it did not happen. Later Krishnaswami visited Mahatma Gandhi in Madras. When he introduced himself as a resident of Ramanashram, the

Mahatma replied, "I would love to come and see Bhagavan but I don't know when the time will come."

Also worth mentioning is the brief visit of Somerset Maugham, the celebrated British writer, which took place in 1939. Major Chadwick was sitting with Maugham on the veranda when he suddenly fainted. He was brought to Chadwick's room to rest. Later Sri Ramana came to see him there. They sat opposite each other for half an hour without a word being said. Then Somerset Maugham asked, "Is there any need to say anything?" "No," replied Sri Ramana, "Silence is best. Silence is itself conversation." About the meeting Somerset Maugham wrote the essay 'The Saint' and also digested his impressions in his famous novel 'The Razor's Edge'.

Sri Ramana took a special interest in newcomers. Devotees often wrote to the Ashram saying which train they would arrive on. The Tiruvannamalai station master reports, "Once, a devotee from Ceylon wrote that he was starting from Colombo on a particular day and would be reaching the Ashram. He forgot to mention the time of his arrival at Tiruvannamalai. So, Bhagavan asked me to find out from available Time Tables when the steamer started from Ceylon, when it reached Dhanushkoti and when he could be expected to reach Tiruvannamalai. Only after I found out the details and told the exact date and time, was He satisfied."[88]

It was the custom at the Ashram that newcomers were given the best places at meals, which were directly opposite the Maharshi. If the stay was prolonged this often turned into the exact opposite and at times Sri Ramana did not even deign to look at them. They were thus prevented from thinking that they had gained his special attention or any preferential treatment.

When devotees visited their master they brought presents with them, mostly in the form of fruits or sweets which would at once be distributed amongst those present. Sometimes disciples would also

---

[88] Ganesan: Moments, p. 85

bring a special, expensive gift for the Maharshi's personal use, but these were not normally welcomed.

Ramana with a visitor from the West

Once someone wanted to give Sri Ramana a silver box which was meant for the nuts for the squirrels. The small sheet metal box used for this purpose looked old and ugly and so the devotee may have thought that this would be a useful gift. But Ramana did not even touch it and replied, "What, a silver box? No. Please take it back. Look at this; a silver box for me!"

When a devotee brought a nice walking stick with a silver handle for Sri Ramana he said jokingly, "Good. It is very nice. Please use it carefully." The disciple replied, "But it is not for my use. I have brought it thinking that Bhagavan would use it." "What an idea!", said Ramana. "A nice walking stick with a silver handle should be used only by officials like you. Why for me? Look, I have my own walking stick. That is enough."

At the beginning of the forties a devotee brought an electric table fan for Ramana. The answer was as usual, "Why this fan? The ordinary fan is there. We have hands. I will fan myself with it whenever necessary. Why do I require all these things?" But the devotee would not leave it at that and argued, "Is it not some trouble? If the electric fan is used there is no trouble whatsoever." But Ramana replied, "What is the trouble? If the ordinary fan is used we get just as much breeze as we want. The electric fan blows too much breeze and with a whizzing noise. Moreover, some electric current is consumed. For that, there will be a bill. Why should we make the office bear that expense on our account?"[89]

The story of the fan was, however, far from over. The devotee simply left it there and it was placed near Ramana's couch. If the weather was very sultry someone would switch it on for Ramana. But he would object, saying, "If you want a fan you can keep it near yourselves." If no one turned it off he did it himself. He also did not want anyone to fan him with an ordinary fan if others could not also enjoy the benefits.

Sri Ramana repeatedly complained about the many things which were offered to him and which he did not actually need, "I am a poor man. For my status, even what I now have is too much. This sofa, these mattresses, these pillows – why all these? You people do not agree, but how happy would it be if I could spread out this towel and sit on the floor!" Mudaliar replied, "You say even that towel should be no bigger than the present one!" Ramana replied," Why a bigger one? It is half-a-yard broad and three-quarters of a yard long. It is sufficient for drying the body after bath, for spreading over the head if you walk in the sun, for tying round the neck if it is cold and for spreading on the floor to sit on. What more could we do with a bigger one?"[90]

---

[89] Nagamma: Letters, pp. 433ff
[90] dto.: p. 435

In the Old Hall

Ramana with devotees

Though Sri Ramana used words sparingly and gave his most profound instruction in silence, there are records of so many talks that they fill whole volumes, not to mention those which were never written down. Almost daily from May 1935 to April 1939 Munagala S. Venkataramiah wrote down visitors' questions and Sri Ramana's answers. These were published under the title 'Talks with Sri Ramana Maharshi'. Devaraja Mudaliar did the same for the period March 1945 to January 1947 in 'Day by Day with Bhagavan' and Suri Nagamma for the period November 1945 to February 1950 in 'Letters from Sri Ramanasramam'. In addition there are several collections of conversations with individuals, which devotees have handed over. One of them is 'Maharshi's Gospel'.

Whenever devotees asked questions, Sri Ramana's answers were always suited to the needs and powers of comprehension of the questioner. He immediately knew with what intention a question had been asked. It should be borne in mind that visitors sometimes came with the sole aim of demonstrating their knowledge or of testing Maharshi's.

Sri Ramana taught the way of Self-enquiry (atma vichara, see also Chapter 18). But for those to whom this did not appeal he would suggest devotion to god (*bhakti*), which leads to the same goal. If someone practised *mantra japa*, yoga or another form of meditation, he would confirm that this was fine, but would gently lead him in the direction of atma vichara. He was open to all religions, so there are many facets to his way of teaching. He never forced anyone to adopt a specific path, but at times he could be very firm.

Sometimes devotees would not ask their questions orally, preferring to write them down on a slip of paper. Once a simple woman had written to him, "I am not learned in the Scriptures and I find the method of Self-enquiry too hard for me. I am a woman with seven children and a lot of household cares, and it leaves me little time for meditation. I request Bhagavan to give me some simpler and easier method."

Sri Ramana gave her the following practical advice, "No learning or knowledge of Scriptures is necessary to know the Self, as no man requires a mirror to see himself. All knowledge is required only to be given up eventually as not-Self. Nor is household work or cares with children necessarily an obstacle. If you can do nothing more, at least continue saying 'I,I' to yourself mentally all the time, as advised in 'Who am I?', whatever work you may be doing and whether you are sitting, standing or walking. 'I' is the name of God. It is the first and greatest of all *mantras*. Even OM is second to it."[91]

A young man asked Maharshi, "Swami, having a great desire for *moksha* (deliverance) and anxious to know the way thereto, I have read all sorts of books on *Vedanta*. They all describe it, each in a different way. I have also visited a number of learned people and

---

[91] Mudaliar: Day by Day, p. 229

when I asked them, each recommended a different path. I got puzzled and have come to you; please tell me which path to take."

Sri Ramana answered with a smile, "All right, then, go the way you came."

The young man was confused and did not know what to say. He waited until Ramana had left the Hall and then turned to the others disheartened saying, "Gentlemen, I have come a long way with great hope and with no regard for the expenses or discomfort, out of my ardent desire to know the way to *moksha*; is it fair to tell me to go the way I came. Is this such a huge joke?"

Thereupon one of them said, "No, Sir. It is no joke. It is the most appropriate reply to your question. Bhagavan's teaching is that the enquiry, 'Who am I?' is the easiest path to *moksha*. You asked him which way 'I' should go, and his saying, 'Go the way you came,' meant that if you investigate and pursue the path from which that 'I' came, you will attain *moksha*."[92]

Over the course of the years and through his contact with learned devotees such as Ganapati Muni and others, Sri Ramana had become well-versed in *Advaita* literature. If specific questions arose, he would take one of the many books from the bookshelf beside his couch and read the appropriate passage from it or give it to the questioner to read. He had an exceptionally good memory and so always knew where to look to find a particular book or the appropriate passage. He recommended reading the *Bhagavad Gita*, the *Ribhu Gita*, the works of *Shankara* such as *Dakshinamurti Stotram*, *Vivekachudamani* and *Atma Bodha*, also *Yoga Vasishta*, *Ashtavakra Gita*, *Ellam Ondre* and *Kaivalya Navaneeta*. He translated into Tamil those parts of these *Advaita* scriptures, which he considered to be especially important.

---

[92] Nagamma: Letters, pp. 16ff

Sri Ramana was also an excellent storyteller. He liked to make use of the stories of the *Periyapuranam* and other spiritual scriptures, with their legends about kings, saints and gods. When telling these stories he used to dramatize the characters of the main figures in voice and gesture and seemed to identify himself fully with them. If the story was particularly moving, he would at times be overcome by such intense emotions, that he was unable to reach the end of the story. Once when reading a very moving story from the *Periyapuranam* about the deep devotion of the saint Kannappar, sweat broke out of all the pores of his body, his hair stood on end and tears flowed from his eyes. He was barely able to speak. All those present in the Hall became silent and one could hear a pin drop. Everyone was speechless that the devotion of the great hunter-saint could cause this great *jnani* to be overcome by such emotions and ecstasy. After a while Ramana silently closed the book, wiped away the tears with the corner of his towel and said that he was unable to go on reading.

The Old Hall was not only the place where spiritual questions were asked and answered, day-to-day problems were also dealt with there. Devotees came to lay their troubles before their master. For long-standing devotees in particular it was natural to come to Sri Ramana with their worries and ask for his help or advice. Whether the coming marriage of a daughter, the birth of a child, a sick family member, professional troubles, financial hardships or even more mundane matters – no matter was considered too insignificant. Ramana reacted to the needs of his devotees with sympathy and helped at times by giving concrete advice. At times, however, he might also direct the devotee's attention along another path. Feroza Taleyarkhan reported the following amusing story, "An Indian gentleman who had spent about a year in Germany and had brought down with him an expensive radio set was rather worried that it was not working and that there was none at hand to set it right. He carried his worries to Bhagavan, perhaps expecting Bhagavan to set the radio right. Little did he (or we) know Bhagavan. In a consoling voice Bhagavan referred to his worries over the radio, its cost, the lack of a mechanic to set it right and so on. Then began something unusual. He said to the visitor that if he tried to tune his own inner radio with eyes closed he could hear and speak to any country in the world and elsewhere too. A peal of laughter shook the Hall then. Little did we realise that the joke was on us too."[93]

The Englishman Arthur Osborne, who joined the Ashram in the late forties and lived there together with his family, describes the vivid bustle in the Hall as follows, "Some of the devotees, without rising from their places, talk with Sri Bhagavan about themselves or their friends, give news of absent devotees, ask doctrinal questions. One feels the homely atmosphere, as of a great family. Perhaps someone has a private matter to report and goes up to the couch to speak to Sri Bhagavan in an undertone or to hand him a paper on which he has written it out. ... A mother brings a little child in and he smiles to it more beautifully than a mother. A little girl brings her doll and makes it prostrate before the couch and then shows it to Bhagavan who takes it and looks at it. A young monkey slips in at the door and tries to grab a banana. The attendant chases it out, but there happens to be only one attendant present, so it runs round the end of the Hall and in through the other door, and Sri Bhagavan whispers urgently to it, 'Hurry! Hurry! He'll be back soon.' A wild-looking *sadhu* with matted locks and ochre robe stands with hands upraised before the couch. A prosperous townsman in European suit makes a decorous prostration and secures a front seat; his companion, not quite sure of his devotion, does not prostrate at all.

A group of pandits [scholars] sit near the couch, translating a Sanskrit work, and from time to time take it up to him to elucidate some point. A three-year-old, not to be outdone, takes up his story of Little Bo Peep, and Sri Bhagavan takes that too, just as graciously, and looks through it with the same interest; but it is tattered, so he passes it to an attendant to bind and gives it back next day neatly repaired."[94]

---

[93] Taleyarkhan: Sages, p. 95
[94] Osborne: Ramana Maharshi and the Path, pp. 129ff

Sadguru Ramana

The literal meaning of Guru is 'one who drives away the darkness of ignorance'. In 'Spiritual Instruction' (Upadesa Manjari) Sri Ramana describes the characteristics of a *Sadguru*, i.e. a perfect *Guru*, as follows, "Steady abidance in the Self, looking at all with an equal eye, unshakable courage at all times, in all places and circumstances." The earnest disciple, however, is marked by "an intense longing for the removal of sorrow and attainment of joy and an intense aversion for all kinds of mundane pleasure."[95]

At the beginning of the traditional master/disciple relationship there is usually an initiation (*diksha*) through touch (laying on hands), *mantra* or look (*darshan*). Sri Ramana officially neither gave any of these forms of initiation, nor ever asserted that he was the Guru of this or that disciple. From his point of view there was neither master nor disciple. So he answered Paul Brunton, who wanted to obtain initiation from him by any means, "What is all this talk of masters

---

[95] Collected Works, p. 53

and disciples? All these differences exist only from the disciple's standpoint. To the one who has realized the true Self there is neither master nor disciple. Such a one regards all people with equal eye."[96]

Likewise Major Chadwick once wanted visible confirmation that he was a disciple of Ramana. The Maharshi turned to another devotee and said humorously, "Ask him, does he want me to give him a written document? Go and call Narayanier, the Sub-Registrar, and tell him to make one out for him." And later he added jokingly, "Go and get the office stamp and put it on him. Will that convince him?"

Nevertheless Sri Ramana was and is the *Sadguru* of many people. His look (*darshan*) was experienced very intensely. For that reason his devotees often experienced and interpreted his *darshan* as a kind of initiation and transmission of grace. Right up until his death Ramana's eyes had an exceptional intense brilliance. It was not rare that he would look at someone for minutes on end or even longer. Louis Hartz reports, "Suddenly the Maharshi looked at me with great intensity. His eyes took possession of me. I don't know how long it lasted, but I felt absolute great inner peace." And Professor Subbaramayya recounts, "As our eyes met, there was a miraculous effect upon my mind. I felt as if I had plunged into a pool of peace."

All his life Sri Ramana resisted being venerated as a Guru. The disciple shows his veneration, for example, by touching the feet of the master. However this was strictly forbidden at Ramanashram.

When Roda McIver felt a deep longing to touch Sri Ramana's feet, he answered, "Why do you want to touch these feet? Bhagavan's feet are over your head." And to another devotee who expressed the desire, to lay his head on his feet, he put the question, "Which is the foot and which is the head?" The devotee knew not what to answer. After a while Maharshi said, "Where the self merges, that is the foot. It is in one's own self. The feeling 'I' 'I', the ego, is the head. Where that ego dissolves, that is the foot of the Guru."

---

[96] Brunton: A Search in Secret India, p. 277

Prostration (*namaskaram*) is also widely used as an expression of veneration for Guru and God. With hands folded above the head the devotee throws himself flat on the ground, face downwards. When devotees entered the Hall, they used to do *namaskaram* to Sri Ramana and occasionally they also overdid it. But the Maharshi repeatedly stressed that the real *namaskaram* is in the heart. When a man prostrated innumerable times to him, he said, "Where is the need for all these gymnastics? It is better to show your devotion by keeping quiet!"

Suri Nagamma reports an amusing incident, which again testifies to Sri Ramana's good sense of humour, "As soon as Bhagavan returned to the Hall and sat on the couch, one of the devotees put some incense into the stove nearby. The fumes were a little too intense and as they spread around Bhagavan's face, he felt almost suffocated. 'Shall we open the windows?' suggested a devotee. Bhagavan said, 'Let it be. Leave it alone. In the temples, we burn the incense and fan the fumes towards the deity so that the idol is completely enveloped in the fumes. Your idea in burning the incense here also is to see that the Swami should enjoy the fumes. Moreover they are spreading out of their own accord. Why are you now trying to drive the fumes away?' Just as Bhagavan was saying this, a devotee fanned the embers in the stove with his hand. Suddenly the whole thing burst into a flame. We were afraid that the heat of the flame might affect Bhagavan and began to feel anxious. But Bhagavan said with a smile, 'Yes, now it is all right. The incense has been burnt and the lights have been waved, the process of *puja* is now complete.'"[97]

Whatever Maharshi touched or used was highly prized by his devotees, as they considered it to be *prasad* and that it passed on some of the power and blessing of the Guru to them. Devotees secretly liked to take the leaf plate from which he had eaten so that they could eat from it themselves, without him knowing about it.

---

[97] Nagamma: Letters and Recollections, p. 113. The waving of the lights means the waving of the camphor lights (arati) as done at the *puja* in front of the statue of the Goddess.

But when he found out, he immediately took precautions so that it could not happen again.

Likewise the water with which he washed his hands after meals was sought after. Not even his bath water was safe from devotees. It is again Suri Nagamma who reports the following fantastic incident, "In the room where Bhagavan takes his bath, there is a hole through which the water that is used drains out. Below that, a gutter was constructed to drain off the water. At the time of his bathing, some devotees used to gather at that place, sprinkle on their heads the water that came out of the room, wipe their eyes and even use it for achamaniyam (sipping drops of water for religious purpose). That was going on quietly and unobserved for some time. But in due course people began bringing vessels and buckets to gather that water and soon there was a regular queue. That naturally resulted in some noise which reached Bhagavan's ears. He enquired and found out the facts. Addressing the attendants, he said, '… What nonsense! Will you get this stopped or shall I bathe at the tap outside? If that is done, you will be saved the trouble of heating water for me, and there will be no trouble for them either, to watch and wait for that tirtha [holy water]. What do I want? Only two things, a towel and a *koupina*. I can bathe and then rinse them at the tap and that completes the job. If not the tap, you have the hill streams and the tanks. Why this bother? What do you say?'"[98] As a result, Chinnaswami immediately put an end to these practices.

From time immemorial the master/disciple relationship has been based on the disciple caring for the physical welfare of his master and performing various tasks for him. In return the Guru bestows his grace upon the disciple. Sri Ramana did not really subscribe to this view. In his opinion the devotee's abidance in the true Self represented true service to the Guru.

Some devotees, who visited the Ashram regularly during their holidays, tended to become involved in various Ashram activities

---

[98] Nagamma: Letters, p. 219

during their stay, which they interpreted as service to their Guru Ramana. If Maharshi noticed that, he would say, "In the name of service to the Guru, they should not waste their time in activities and become disappointed later." And if someone complained that they could not find sufficient time for meditation he would say, "Is it that you have got no time for meditation? Or is it that you are unable to remain quiet? If you can remain quiet, go ahead and do so! You will then see how all the Ashram activities go on naturally of their own accord."

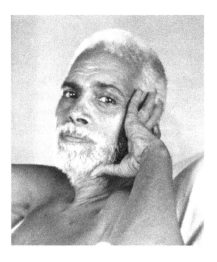

Once a devotee from the West was clearing away the leaf plates in front of the dining hall, which was a completely useless occupation, as the used leaves were in any case meant to be thrown away. When Ramana saw him, he asked him why he was doing it. The devotee answered that he had not found any means to be of service since his arrival at the Ashram, so he wanted to do this work. But Ramana replied indignantly, "Is sweeping the used leaf plates the means to get salvation? Is it to perform this *tapas* that you have come here all the way from abroad. Go! Go! Enough of doing this kind of service! Go inside, sit to one side, turn your mind inward and find out he who wants to be saved. The service of purifying your heart is alone the highest service. That alone can truly redeem you." [99]

Sri Ramana made no distinctions between his devotees. Whether they lived with him, came to visit now and then or even if they never saw him at all in the body, his grace flowed and continues to flow for all of them. He would say, "To me there is no distinction. Grace is flowing like the ocean ever full. Every one draws from it according to his capacity. How can one who brings only a tumbler complain that he is not able to take as much as another who has brought a jar?" [100]

But again and again his devotees would complain that, in their opinion, they were making no spiritual progress. Devaraja Mudaliar, who wrote the famous diary 'Day by Day with Bhagavan', did this particularly often. When one day he was again pestering Ramana about his inability to get rid of his worldly desires, he received the answer, "How do you know?" And at another time Ramana said to him, "Your business is simply to surrender and leave everything to me. If one really surrenders completely, there is no room for him to complain that the Guru has not done this or that."

Some devotees thought that Sri Ramana could give them liberation (*moksha*). He explained to them that he had no bundles of liberation to offer, which he could hand out on demand, "I should give them *moksha*, they say. It is enough if *moksha* alone is given to them. Is not that itself a desire? If you give up all the desires that you have, what remains is only *moksha*."

It is reported that Sri Ramana appeared to some devotees in the form of God or light. His mother once saw Ramana as *Shiva*, with a garland of snakes, then again she saw him in the form of light. Ganapati Muni and others had different visions of him too. When Roda McIver met Maharshi for the first time, he appeared to her as a splendid light. She reports, "Bhagavan had gone up the hill when I

---

[99] Godman: Presence, pp. 115ff
[100] Subbaramayya: Reminiscences, p. 67

arrived, and I was told to wait on the footpath for His return. I did not see Him coming, but suddenly I saw a brilliant light before me, like the sun rising. I lifted my head and saw Bhagavan standing before me. He looked at me, nodded and smiled. At that moment I felt something happening in me which I had never experienced before in my life! The Sun that He was, He revealed at that moment that He was the Light, the Fire of Knowledge!"[101]

When devotees told Sri Ramana about their visions, he would warn them not to attach too much importance to them.

It is also reported that people were healed in the presence of the Maharshi. As, for example, a little boy, whose name was also Ramana and who had been bitten by some kind of poisonous animal. When the parents brought the boy to the Maharshi he was already unconscious and had almost stopped breathing. Sri Ramana passed his hands over the boy's body saying, "It is nothing. He will be all right." And indeed, little Ramana soon recovered.

M.A. Piggot reports a similar occurrence. Someone had brought a man into the Hall who had been bitten by a snake and lay him down before Sri Ramana. "We all watched, fear gripping our hearts. Not so he, who sat looking into the far distance while the victim writhed in pain. Calm and compassion was in that look, and infinite peace. After what seemed like hours, the twitching ceased and the man appeared to sleep. Then the one who had brought in the sufferer gently touched him. The man rose, prostrated himself before the Maharshi and went out cured."[102]

Such spectacular incidents were, however, rare. Mostly Ramana kept silent if people tried to claim that he had healed someone.

---

[101] Ganesan: Moments, p. 38
[102] Piggot: The Way of the Spirit. In: The Maharshi, July/August 1999, p. 4

14. Sri Ramana and the Animals

De Acosta: "Does one who has realised the Self lose the sense of 'I'?"

Ramana: "Absolutely."

De Acosta: "Then there is no difference between yourself and myself, that man over there, my servant. Are all the same?"

Ramana: "All are the same, including those monkeys."

De Acosta: "But the monkeys are not people. Are they not different?"

Ramana: "They are exactly the same as people. All are the same in One Consciousness."

The Maharshi was attentive to the needs of all living things. He could communicate with them, understand their reactions and build up true relationships with them. He offered his protection to all animals. For him they were equal to, and had the same rights as, humans and he often reacted angrily if his devotees did not respect them. He treated them as if they were his devotees and was always considerate towards them. He never referred to any animal as 'it', but always said 'he' or 'she'. Whenever anybody tried to drive the monkeys, birds, squirrels, dogs, cats or snakes away, he defended them saying, "We do not know who they are. … You merely see the skin that covers the body but not the person that is within. You feel that you are great, and the others are small, and so try to drive them away. They have come here just as we have come. Why do they not have the same rights that we have?"[103] In return the animals felt strongly drawn towards him.

---

[103] Nagamma: Letters, p. 424

Wild Animals and Plants

One day a female leopard came to the watering place near the Virupaksha Cave. The frightened devotees beat upon their plates and drums to drive her away. But she quenched her thirst unconcerned and then went on her way with a roar. Ramana said astonished, "Why do you worry so much? The leopard intimated to me by the first roar that she was coming here. After drinking water she told me by another roar that she was going. She went her own way. She never meddled with your affairs. Why are you so scared? This mountain is the home of these wild animals, and we are their guests. That being so, is it right on your part to drive them away?"[104]

Ramana was equally fearless with regard to scorpions. Vasudeva Sastri recounts, "One day, when we were at Skandashram, I was aghast to find a scorpion climbing up over Bhagavan's body in the front and another at the same time climbing down his back. I was terrified and wanted to do something. But Bhagavan remained calm, as if nothing happened, and the two scorpions, after crawling over his body as if over a wall, eventually left him. After they left, Bhagavan explained to us, 'They crawl over you just as they would crawl on the floor or a wall or tree. Do they crawl over these, stinging as they go? It is only because you fear them and do something, that they fear you and do something in return'."[105]

Sri Ramana defended all living things, including snakes. When Chinnaswami and others noticed a snake on the Ashram premises near the Hall, they shouted out, "What kind of snake is it? Beat it! Beat it!" When Ramana heard the noise of the beating he cried out, "Who is beating it?" But his protests went unnoticed by the party and they killed the snake. He commented afterwards, "If these persons are beaten like that, then they will know what it means."

One day, during the time in the Virupaksha Cave, Ramana was stung by hornets when he inadvertently stepped on their nest. He

---

[104] dto., p. 26
[105] Mudaliar: Day by Day, p. 277

reports, "As I was walking in the bed of a hillstream, I saw a big banyan tree on a boulder, with big leaves, and crossing the stream I wanted to get to the other bank and view from there this big tree. When I accidentally put my left foot near a bush on the way to the other bank, the hornets clustered round my left leg up to the knee and went on stinging. They never did anything to my right leg. I left the left leg there for some time, so that the hornets could inflict full punishment on the leg which had encroached on their domain. After a time, the hornets withdrew and I walked on. The leg got swollen very much and I walked with difficulty and reached 'Ezhu Sunai' (Seven Springs) about 2 a.m., and Jadaswami, who was camping there then, gave me some buttermilk mixed with jaggery."[106] When Ramana returned to the Virupaksha Cave he was attended by Palaniswami who carefully drew each sting out of the left leg and rubbed it with oil.

However, in so far as concerns insects which were a nuisance to people, Sri Ramana did not object to killing them. When once a whole army of black ants invaded the Hall through the water drain, he told Annamalai Swami to detect where they were coming from and to put an end to it. The hole was cemented over without further ado. He also used to pluck blood-sucking insects out of the coats of the dogs and throw them into the gleaming coals. Similarly he did not object if devotees killed mosquitoes or used insecticide in the cowshed.

Maharshi had the same compassionate attitude towards plants as towards animals. One day workers had been deputed to gather mangoes from one of the trees. But instead of climbing up the tree and picking them one by one, they knocked them down with sticks. In this way a large number of leaves were knocked down along with the fruit. Ramana, who was as usual sitting in the Hall, heard the beating and sent a message via his attendants that it should stop at once. When he later passed by the tree and saw the mango leaves in heaps on the floor, he cried out harshly, "In return for giving us

---

[106] dto., p. 187

fruit, is the tree to be beaten with sticks? Who gave you this work? Instead of beating the tree, you might as well cut it to the roots. You need not gather the fruit. Go away!"

Sundaresa Iyer reports a similar incident, "One morning K. was cutting down the ripe coconuts from the trees while Bhagavan was returning from the cowshed. Bhagavan asked K. what rod he was using to pluck the coconuts, whether it had a bamboo bit attached to the end or an iron point. K. remarked that it was only an iron sickle. Bhagavan asked, 'Will not the trees be hurt by the sharp iron? Would not a rod with a bamboo bit at the end serve the purpose?' But he did not wait for a reply. K. went on with his work without changing his implement. He continued to use the same iron sickle every morning.

A week later, at the same time as on the previous occasion, while K. was cutting down the coconuts from the trees, one fell on his forehead, striking his nose very painfully. This news was reported to Bhagavan. While expressing pity for the man, Bhagavan also remarked, 'Now he will know what it is to be hurt, and also how much his iron sickle must have hurt the uncomplaining trees.'"[107]

Monkeys

There were large bands of monkeys living on Arunachala. Sri Ramana had had dealings with them since the time when he lived in the Virupaksha Cave and this did not change when he settled down at the foot of the hill in Ramanashram. He had studied their behaviour and knew everything about the hierarchical structure of a monkey tribe and its laws. He knew what they preferred and understood their speech. He often defended their behaviour and activities and sometimes also compared them with those of people, often to the detriment of the latter. He became very friendly with some of the monkeys, such as, for example, Nandi (the Lame), a

---

[107] Sundaresa Iyer: At the Feet, p. 33

name which he had given to a monkey which had become lame. Nandi had been bitten by the monkey king and left, badly injured, to die near the Virupaksha Cave. Ramana was moved by compassion and cared for him until he regained his health. Thereafter Nandi was deeply attached to Ramana and always stayed close to him. He now received his daily food from the Ashram and if other monkeys came by, he prevented them from approaching Ramana. Later Nandi himself became the monkey king.

Ramana with monkey

Ramana defended the monkeys and their actions at each opportunity. Sometimes they created havoc with the food and other things which devotees had brought. If someone complained to him he would say, "Not many years back it was deep jungle here, the monkeys' home. We came, cleared the ground, built houses and drove the monkeys away. Who is to blame, we or they? If they give us a little trouble, can we not bear it quietly?"

When one of the attendants beat the monkeys, because they had stolen nuts, Bhagavan rebuked him, "You are not beating the monkeys, you are beating me. The pain is mine."

The monkeys often stole the fruit which devotees had brought as a food offering, if the latter were not careful or were meditating. One of the attendants was entrusted with the task of receiving the fruit from the visitors. One day he was sitting with eyes closed, a basket full of fruit at his side, listening to the radio. In the meantime the monkeys were freely helping themselves to the contents of the basket. When people in the Hall tried to chase the monkeys away, Ramana joked, "When these attendants are immersed in deep meditation, the monkeys come and see to the work of the attendants. Someone has to look after the work! The attendants put the fruit into the basket, the monkeys put the fruit into their stomachs; that is all the difference. While people forget themselves while listening to the music over the radio the monkeys busy themselves in enjoying the sweet juice of the fruit. That is good, isn't it!"

The monkey mothers liked to come with their babies, to show them to Ramana full of pride. Suri Nagamma reports, "Yesterday a monkey with her baby stood in the window by the side of Bhagavan's sofa. Bhagavan was reading something and so did not notice it. After a while, the monkey screeched and one of the attendants tried to drive her away by shouting, but she would not go. Bhagavan then looked up and said, 'Wait! She has come here to show her baby to Bhagavan; do not all the people bring their children to show them? For her, her child is equally dear. Look how young that child is.' So saying, Bhagavan turned towards her, and said in an endearing tone, 'Hullo! So you have brought your child? That is good!' And, giving her a plantain, he sent her away."[108]

Sri Ramana felt a deep admiration for the monkey tribes and was convinced that *tapas* was not unknown to them. Once he said, "I have known something about their organisation, their kings, laws,

---

[108] Nagamma: Letters, p. 262

153

regulations. Everything is so perfect and well-organised. So much intelligence behind it all. I even know that *tapas* is not unknown to monkeys. A monkey whom we used to call 'Mottaipaiyan' was once oppressed and ill-treated by a gang. He went away into the forest for a few days, did *tapas*, acquired strength and returned. When he came and sat on a bough and shook it, all the rest of the monkeys, who had previously ill-treated him and of whom he was previously mortally afraid, were now quaking before him. Yes, I am clear that *tapas* is well known to monkeys."[109]

On festival days monkeys were always looked after and were given a special meal from the festival offerings.

Squirrels and Sparrows

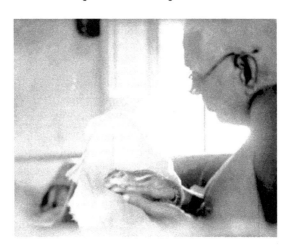

Ramana with squirrel

Squirrels and sparrows liked to build their nests near Sri Ramana. He remembers, "There was once a regular war between the people here and the squirrels for a whole month. They used to build their nests over my head. Each day the people would destroy them and

---

[109] Mudaliar: Day by Day, pp. 138ff

the next day the squirrels would have built them again. At last all the holes in the roof were stopped up and the squirrels could do nothing. At one time they used to run all over my couch and get into the sides and under the pillows and everywhere, and I had to look carefully before I sat down or leaned back. It has sometimes happened that I have accidentally leaned heavily on some small squirrel and given it *samadhi* [death] without knowing. The same thing sometimes happened on the hill too, at Skandashram. There too the squirrels used to nestle in my mattress and pillows. It began even before that. Even when I was at Gurumurtam birds and squirrels used to build their nests all round me."[110]

One day when Ramana inadvertently bumped against a sparrow's nest, an egg fell out and cracked. He was dismayed and cried out to his attendant Madhava, "Look, look what I have done today! Oh, the poor mother will be so sorrow-stricken, perhaps angry with me also, at my causing the destruction of her expected little one! Can the cracked eggshell be pieced together again? Let us try!"

So saying he took a piece of wet cloth, wrapped it around the broken egg and laid it back into its nest. Each third hour he took it out again, removed the cloth, took it in his hand and glanced at it for a few minutes. Seven days later, after taking the egg from its nest, he announced with the astonishment of a schoolboy, "Look what a wonder! The crack has closed." Some days later he found the egg hatched out, the little bird had come out. With a face beaming with joy he took the nestling into his hand, stroked and caressed it and handed it to the others, that they could also admire it.

One day some new born squirrels had fallen out of their nest and landed on Ramana's couch. Their eyes were still closed and they were very tiny. The mother, however, did not take them back. But how should one feed such tiny things? The squirrels laid in Ramana's palm. His face was glowing with love and affection towards them. The devotees looked on helplessly, but he was happy

---

[110] dto., p. 234

and cheerful. He asked for some cotton and made a soft bed for them. Then he took a piece of the cotton, rolled it up so that the end looked like a sharp needle, dipped it into some milk and trickled it in their tiny mouths. This he did repeatedly. He looked after them with great care and love until they grew up and started running around. They did not run away, however, but always ran around their 'mother'.

Something similar happened, when a cat ate the mother of some young squirrels. Again Ramana took on the task of caring for the young. As he liked to use daily events to teach his devotees he said to them, "These little ones do not know that wisdom lies in remaining in their nest. They keep attempting to come out. All trouble lies outside but they cannot remain within. Similarly if the mind is not externalised, but remains sunk in the Heart then there would only be happiness. But the mind keeps moving out." When Rangaswami asked, "What is the path for keeping it inward?", Bhagavan said, "It is exactly the same as what I am doing now. Each time a young squirrel comes out, I keep putting it back into its nest. When I go on doing it, it learns the happiness of staying in the nest."[111]

The Cow Lakshmi

Many animals used to live in the Ashram. There are several animal *samadhis* (graves) on the Ashram premises, which continue to be honoured even today. The stories about the white peacock, Valli the deer and Jackie the dog are well-known. But the most famous Ashram animal was the cow Lakshmi.

In 1926 a certain Arunachala Pillai presented a cow and her calf to Sri Ramana as a gift. At first Ramana refused to accept them as the Ashram did not have the necessary facilities for the animals to be cared for properly. The donor was asked to take them back again.

---

[111] Unforgettable Years, pp. 53ff

But the devotee insisted that the cow and calf be left with Ramana. Finally Ramanatha Dikshitar, who lived near the Ashram, promised to look after the animals. Three months later they were transferred to the care of Pasupathi Aiyar, who lived in town.

Ramana with Lakshmi

A year later Pasupathi Aiyar came to have Sri Ramana's *darshan* and brought the cow and calf to show him. The calf, however, remembered the way to the Ashram and next morning it came to Ramana all by itself. Thereafter it would come each morning, spend the day at the Ashram and return to town in the evening by itself. Ramana was very friendly towards it and gave it all kinds of delicacies to eat. Many years passed in this way. The calf naturally grew into a cow and was named 'Lakshmi'.

The Maharshi said about Lakshmi, that even though she could not speak, she understood everything and reacted as intelligently as a human being.

Punctually at mealtimes Lakshmi would enter the Hall and accompany Ramana to the dining hall. The natural manner with which she asserted her claims on him and the great friendliness with which he treated her, led devotees to speculate about Lakshmi's connection to Maharshi in an earlier life, but Ramana never said anything on the matter.

In the course of her lifetime Lakshmi gave birth to nine calves. Three of them were born on Ramana's birthday. Later she and her calves were allowed to stay at the Ashram itself.

Shantamma reports, "Once Lakshmi came into the Hall. She was pregnant at that time. It was after lunch time, when Bhagavan was reading the newspapers. Lakshmi came near and started licking the papers. Bhagavan looked up and said: 'Wait a little, Lakshmi.' But Lakshmi went on licking. Bhagavan laid his paper aside, put his hands behind Lakshmi's horns and his head against hers. Like this they stayed for quite a long time. I stood nearby looking at the wonderful scene. After some ten minutes or so, Bhagavan turned to me and said: 'Do you know what Lakshmi is doing? She is in *samadhi*.' I looked at her and tears were flowing in streams down her broad cheeks. Her breathing had stopped and her eyes were fixed on Bhagavan. After some time Bhagavan changed his position and asked: 'Lakshmi, how do you feel now?' Lakshmi moved backwards, as if reluctant to turn her tail towards Bhagavan, walked round the Hall and went out."[112]

As the Ashram grew, the number of cattle which were kept there also grew. A stone cowshed (goshala) had to be built. On the ceremonial opening day Lakshmi was supposed to enter the new cowshed first. She had been bathed and decorated, but she escaped, went to Ramana and stood in front of him. She would not move from there until he stood up and went over to the cowshed. So he was the first one to enter her new house, and she followed him.

On 17th June 1948 Lakshmi fell ill. The following morning Ramana went to her and said, "Amma (mother), do you want me to be near

---

[112] Shantamma: Eternal Bhagavan. In: Ramana Smrti, pp.[84ff]

you now?" He looked into her eyes, laid one of his hands on her head, the other one on her Heart and stroked her. He laid his cheek on her face. When he was sure that her Heart was pure, without any passion (*vasanas*) and fully concentrated on him, he left her and went back to the Hall. Shortly before her end she licked some sweet rice. Her eyes were calm and peaceful. She remained conscious until the last and died peacefully at half past eleven.

Ramana had given liberation to both his mother and Lakshmi. She was buried with all due ceremonies and a *samadhi* was created for her near the other animal graves. On her gravestone it reads, "On 18.6.1948 the cow Lakshmi attained liberation (*mukti*)."

Other Ashram Animals

One day devotees brought a deer named Valli to the Ashram. Again Ramana did not want to accept it at first. Finally Madhava Swami said he was willing to look after the deer and so it was allowed to stay. It soon became the darling of the Ashram. Annamalai Swami relates, "Valli often came to the Hall and put her forehead on the soles of Bhagavan's feet. Sometimes when she did this Bhagavan would play with her by pushing his feet strongly against her head. Valli would respond by playfully butting Bhagavan's feet. At other times, when Valli danced on her hind legs, Bhagavan would stand alongside her, imitating her actions by dancing with his feet and waving his arms."[113]

One day Valli disappeared. A search was organized and she was found injured with a broken leg. She was bandaged and placed in a corner of the old dining room, but she did not have long to live. Shortly before her death Sri Ramana sat at her side. He laid one of his hands on her head and with the other one touched her Heart and kept both hands in this position for more than one hour. He stayed at her side until she died at around five p.m. Ramana helped

---

[113] Godman: Living by the Words, p. 82

Annamalai Swami to build a small shrine for Valli near the back door of the Ashram.

Ramana with the white peacock

Another well-known Ashram animal was the white peacock. He was presented in April 1947 as a gift from the Rani of Baroda.

When Ramana saw him he said, "Isn't it enough that ten or twelve coloured peacocks are here? They may come to fight with this one because it is of a different variety. Besides that it has to be protected against attacks of cats. Why this? It is better to send it back to its own place." The person who had brought it, however, took no notice and simply left the peacock there. It was decided that Krishnaswami should care for it.

Once when the peacock ran away, Krishnaswami caught it and brought it back. Ramana soothing laid his hand on its neck saying, "You naughty chap, where did you go? How can we manage to look after you, if you go away like this? Please don't. There will be cruel animals elsewhere. Why not stay on here?" Thus he persuaded it. The peacock did not run away anymore but instead liked to walk

160

about the Ashram premises. Each day he would visit the site where the Temple for the Mother was being built, so Ramana jokingly called him 'supervisor'. Sometimes he strutted along the queues of people eating in the dining hall and so received the title 'the *sarvadhikari's* assistant'.

The peacock had its perch near Ramana's couch and it also slept there at night. Ramana took great care of it, plucked lice out of its feathers and taught it not to eat insects and caterpillars but to feed itself on vegetarian food only.

The Old Hall had by now become too small, so Ramana usually sat in the open Jubilee Hall. He also slept there outside in summer. The peacock made a lot of mess, so a cage was built for it and installed in the Jubilee Hall near Ramana's couch. The management decided that in winter the animal should stay outside at night, whereas Ramana was meant to sleep in the warm Old Hall. But Ramana refused saying, "The peacock came to us from somewhere. What respect is it to that guest if we make him sleep outside while we sleep inside? If a relative comes to your house, is it proper to make him sleep on the veranda while you sleep inside the house?" And he made the point by staying outside in the Jubilee Hall together with the white peacock for the next two nights.

The rumour circulated in the Ashram that the white peacock was a reincarnation of Sri Ramana's former longstanding attendant Madhava Swami, as the peacock displayed similar patterns of behaviour. It had been one of Madhava Swami's duties to repair books and re-bind them. When the peacock made its rounds, it often pecked at the books which Madhava had given a new binding to, leaving the others untouched. The peacock also did not like to have anything to do with females of its species, as had been the case with Madhava Swami. It also liked to lie down in his former favourite place. For that reason Ramana also called it 'Madhava'.

On the night Sri Ramana died the white peacock sat on the roof of the room in which he was dying and screeched continuously.

Several dogs lived in the Ashram. The most famous was Jackie, who was later buried in the Ashram compound alongside the deer Valli and a crow. He did not much like playing and did not join the other dogs, but would sit in front of Sri Ramana, fixing his gaze on his eyes incessantly. He would also not start eating until Ramana had taken a mouthful of food. One day when a stray dog entered the Ashram through the back door, Jackie started barking. Ramana calmed him saying, "You just close your eyes. You just close your eyes. You just close your eyes. If you do this you will not be able to see the dog." At once Jackie closed his eyes.

One day Jackie was attacked by a ferocious pig and was seriously injured. His stomach was torn open and the intestines came out. It required a lot of stitches to close it up and afterwards Jackie was carried to a *mantapam* opposite the Ashram to recover. At the same time Kunju Swami was suffering from a severe abscess on his foot and was also staying in the same *mantapam*. When Sri Ramana came to visit them, Kunju Swami was crying out in pain and fell at Maharshi's feet. But Ramana said to him, "See, how Jackie is silently bearing his pain after such a major operation, without so much as a whimper!" This was helpful to Kunju Swami and his pain became bearable for him. Ramana stroked Jackie and enquired if the meal had been brought and then left both patients.

Jackie also died in Sri Ramana's arms.

15. The Later Years

Seeing the world, the jnani sees the Self which is the substratum of all that is seen; the ajnani, whether he sees the world or not, is ignorant of his true Being, the Self.

Poor Health

Sri Ramana's health was never particularly good. His head used to shake and in the later years he always used a walking stick to get about. He also looked older than he was. When once Kunju Swami mentioned the matter to him he replied, "What is there so strange in it? If a big elephant is tied down in a small hut, what else happens to that hut except troubles of all sorts? This is the same."

As time passed he became increasingly weak and suffered from severe rheumatism. The devotees did their best to provide relief, mainly in the form of massage with a variety of oils.

Dr. Srinivasa Rao once said, "You are always in a reclining posture. It is bound to be painful for the body. A little massage would be a great relief." Ramana answered, "I cannot allow these things. How do you know that I am having some pain?" As the doctor did not give way, the Maharshi replied, "If you think that Ramana is the body stretched out on the couch you may ask the body, if the body is feeling the pain then let it answer by itself. If you go on doing this there would be no end to the attention paid to the body." To satisfy him Ramana finally let him massage his legs, but said after a few minutes, "Let me also earn some merit [through service for the guru] by massaging my legs."[114] He then continued to massage his legs himself. He liked to joke in this way whenever devotees wanted to massage him. He would let them do it for a while, but then he would take over himself.

The rheumatism gradually spread to his back and shoulders. In addition, a general state of weakness was evident, although he himself took no notice of it. He was in urgent need of more nourishing food, but would not agree to special food being prepared for him.

Ramachandra Rao, an ayurvedic healer and devotee, wanted to prepare a special tonic for him and wrote a long list with all the ingredients and presented it to Ramana. The Maharshi went through it with interest, but then said that he had not the money to buy such expensive things. "If that medicine is good for me, it must necessarily be good for all the others here. Can you give it to them also as well as to me? If people who do physical work don't need a body-building tonic, how do I who merely sits here and eats? No, no, that can't be!"

In 1942 Ramana had a bad fall. A dog was chasing a squirrel and he wanted to hold the dog back and so stretched out his walking stick, as a result he slipped and broke his collarbone.

---

[114] Unforgettable Years, pp. 151ff

The Golden Jubilee

On 1st September 1946 a huge festival was organized to celebrate the 50th anniversary of Sri Ramana's arrival at Tiruvannamalai. Space in the Old Hall was limited, so it was decided to build a large open hall (pandal) for the occasion on the northern side of the Old Hall, with a roof made of palm leaves. This hall is the previously mentioned Jubilee Hall, which Ramana found very pleasant. The program for the celebration was particularly full and required a great deal of preparation. There were talks by many famous personalities, plus recitals by well-known musicians.

The devotees and the Ashram management had spared no efforts. When the marathon twelve-hour program was shown to Ramana, he said, "It is stated that all these big people will deliver lectures! What about? What is there to speak about? That which is, is *mouna* (silence). How can *mouna* be explained in words? In English, in Sanskrit, in Tamil, in Telugu. Oh, what an array of languages! Eminent people will speak in so many languages! All right! Why should I bother! It is enough if I am not asked to speak."

When the devotee who had presented the program to him, suggested that it could be shortened, he answered smiling, "Have I asked for any of these items, so that I could now object to any one of them? Do what you like. It is all a series of lectures. I will sit like this on the sofa. You may do whatever you like."[115] And so it happened. Sri Ramana remained seated all day long giving *darshan* and went without his midday siesta.

---

[115] Nagamma: Letters, pp. 81ff

In the New Hall

Ramana in the New Hall

During the final years the Old Hall became too small to receive the large numbers of visitors. So the daily *darshan* was now given in the open Jubilee Hall. In 1949 the construction of a new, bigger and well-ventilated hall was completed, along with the Temple of the Mother, and Ramana moved in. But he did not appear to be comfortable in this New Hall. He was particularly sorry that his friends, the animals, no longer had free access. "How can the squirrels come here?", he asked looking up at the ceiling which gave no opportunity for the animals to come in. A devotee answered, "The *sarvadhikari* and others feel that if Bhagavan is here he will be protected from rain or hot sunshine outside." Ramana continued staring at the ceiling and answered with a quavering voice, "If we look for our comfort, is it not at the expense of the sufferings of others? Squirrels, monkeys, peacocks, cows and others have no chance of coming here. Does it not mean that we have deprived them all of their privileges? People think that it is a great happiness for Swami if he is here. What is to be done?" And in the evening, when it was time to feed the animals, he said to his attendant, "They may perhaps think that Swami has given them the slip and gone elsewhere. Please go. What a pity! Go, give them at least some food and come back." And when the attendant returned, he asked concerned, "Have you fed them all? They will perhaps feel that Swami has deserted them and has gone away to a better place and is sitting there so that he alone can be happy. Perhaps they thought that I had forgotten them." [116]

Above all poor people hesitated to enter this magnificent hall and instead would peep embarrassed through the window. Ramana noticing this said, "Rich people are accustomed to see huge buildings with lights, fans, collapsible doors and other imposing furnishings, and so they come inside unhesitatingly. But poor people like me will hesitate to come in, for they feel that it is a place where only rich people live. They are afraid of what people would say if they come in, and so, go away quietly like those people who, as you see, are peeping through the windows. Where is the place for them here? See those poor people! What a pity!" [117]

In the New Hall devotees had installed a stone couch with a thick mattress and side cushions for him. This new mattress was slippery. On one side there was a large cushion for his arm, with another on the back and a third for his feet. Consequently there was little space left for him to sit on. When Sri Ramana sat on the couch for the first time he pressed his hands against it and said to his attendants, "See how this mattress slips from one side to another! People think that it will be comfortable for Bhagavan if there is a costly mattress. It is, however, not possible to sit on this restfully. Why this? It will be much more comfortable if I sit on the stone seat itself."

The following day the mattress was removed and the old one was laid on his couch.

Ramana was, however, not destined to live very long in the New Hall. Only nine months later, in January 1950, he became critically

---

[116] dto., pp. 422ff
[117] dto.

ill and moved to the small Nirvana room, where he was to die the following April.

Political Events

When one considers the momentous political events which occurred during this decade in particular, both in India and throughout the rest of the world, it is surprising what a small part they played in the life of the Maharshi and the Ashram. For example, in 1939 India entered the Second World War and on 15th August 1947 Mahatma Gandhi's non-violent resistance movement against British colonial power finally achieved its aim of Independence for India.

Sri Ramana always read the newspapers and he and his devotees listened to the news on the radio. Occasionally politics were discussed in the Hall. Professor Subbaramayya reports the following interesting conversation, "It was June 10, 1940. The radio announced the fall of Paris to Germany and the entry of Italy into the war against the Allies. ... I had just heard a rumour that to counteract the action of Italy, Turkey had declared war on the side of the Allies. I asked Narayana Iyer, who was the latest arrival from the town whether he had heard any such announcement on the radio. Before Narayana Iyer could reply, Sri Bhagavan Himself said 'No, it cannot be true.' Narayana Iyer confirmed this rare reply of Sri Bhagavan, and turning to me, observed 'France, a first-rate Power has fallen in three days, Then do you think our Britain can hold out longer than three weeks at the most?' Upon this, Sri Bhagavan again observed 'Um! – but Russia – ' Abruptly Sri Bhagavan cut short his speech and resumed silence. Neither of us had the courage to ask Sri Bhagavan what Russia was going to do, though it appeared strange that Sri Bhagavan should mention Russia who was at that time friendly to Germany. It will be remembered that war broke out between Germany and Russia only one year afterwards, and it was in fact Germany's attack on Russia that turned the tide of fortune in favour of the Allies."[118]

When on 30th January 1948 Mahatma Gandhi was assassinated in New Delhi, the whole of India went into mourning. A newspaper reporter came to the Ashram to ask the Maharshi his opinion about the tragedy. Ramana said with a shaking voice, "For the Mahatma's death in this tragic manner, every person's heart is mourning. What is there in particular that I could say? Who is there who is not grieved? If I say anything, you will publish it and then, one after another, people will come and ask me. What is the good of it?" With these words he sent the reporter away and went for his walk. At half past four the women sang 'Raghupati Raghava Rajaram' (one of Mahatma Gandhi's favourite songs). With tears in his eyes Ramana indicated that they should continue with the singing. At 5 p.m. a conch was blown and an arati-celebration (waving of lights) was held in the Mother's Temple for the death of the Mahatma.

After Gandhi's assassination the whole country was plunged into turmoil. There were arson attacks and murders everywhere. The radio in the Hall reported that the situation was very serious. In Tiruvannamalai too people were worried and the town was placed under police guard. Sri Ramana's grand nephew V. Ganesan reports, "It was 9.30 in the morning. Suddenly loud cries of 'Catch them, kill them' were heard. One mad crowd was chasing another and all of them entered the Ashram from the hill-side. There was panic inside the Ashram. A devotee in the Old Hall rushed to the doors and bolted them; the meditating devotees were naturally disturbed. In the midst of all the tense commotion, Bhagavan was unperturbed, a picture of attention, correcting some proof."[119]

---

[118] Subbaramayya: Reminiscences, pp. 77ff
[119] Purushottama Ramana, p. [16]

16. The Fatal Illness

They take this body for Bhagavan and attribute suffering to him. What a pity! They are despondent that Bhagavan is going to leave them and go away; where can he go, and how?

When in early 1949 Sri Ramana was diagnosed as having an incurable cancer, the long death struggle started, not for Sri Ramana, but for the devotees, because the people who really suffered and struggled to maintain his body were his devotees, not he himself. Although there was pain, it was not his pain. The fear of death had left him completely with his experience of enlightenment in Madurai. The death of the body was for him nothing more than the laying down of a burden. For his devotees, however, the thought of losing their master was unbearable. They therefore did everything in their power to try and prolong his life. They begged him repeatedly to heal himself and for a long time refused to accept that his end was near. The conflicting emotions of hope and despair alternated within them, until even the most reluctant was forced to accept that Ramana would soon die.

In this tumult of emotions he acted as a calming influence, repeatedly explaining to his devotees that they were the victims of a misconception, as he was not the body, but the eternal and unchanging Self. So where could he go? What change could there be in his presence and under his guidance? Why this desperate struggle for the body, which was in any case destined to be relinquished at the allotted hour? The full understanding of this truth could only develop within them gradually. As testimony to this we have the deeply moving accounts of those disciples who were in close contact with him and who experienced first-hand the last months of his life, such as S.S. Cohen, Suri Nagamma, Major Chadwick and Arthur Osborne, to name but a few.

Four Operations

The first signs of Ramana's illness appeared in early 1949, when he would often rub his left elbow. An attendant who examined the spot found a boil the size of a pea, which rapidly grew and was soon as big as a marble. Although it seemed to be harmless it was nevertheless removed on 9th February by the Ashram doctor Dr. Shankar Rao and the retired surgeon Dr. Srinivasa Rao, without consulting any other doctors. The operation was performed in the bathroom before breakfast.

Suri Nagamma reports that Sri Ramana would have preferred it if there had been no operation and the ulcer had been left as it was. He said, "It does not give me any pain. Let it be as it is. Why meddle with it?" When the doctor explained, that the problem would be over if the growth was removed, he commented meaningfully, "Oh! Will it be over?"

After the operation Ramana did his best to hide the wound with his towel. When people asked what he had on his arm, he joked, "I am wearing a bracelet" or "A *lingam* is born." The wound took about ten days to heal.

It was not long, however, before another, larger and more painful growth appeared. Renowned doctors from Madras were consulted and they diagnosed it as a malignant tumour.

At the beginning of April 1949 Sri Ramana was again operated upon, this time by Dr. Raghavachari from Madras, in the dispensary. He cut more deeply than was done during the first operation. A detailed examination revealed that it was a sarcoma. The decision was taken to try radium treatment. This second wound had not had time to heal before a third growth appeared.

Samuel S. Cohen[120] was keeping a detailed diary at the time. On 20th April his entry was, "Sri Maharshi's health is causing grave anxiety to the three doctors, who have been in constant attendance on him, as well as to the devotees. A lady devotee wept much and went to him in tears and asked him to give her his disease and be cured of it, saying: 'Bhagavan, you who are curing others must cure yourself and spare your life for us, your devotees.' Once, twice he waved her off, and, seeing her great concern finally replied with great tenderness: 'Why are you so much attached to this body? Let it go.'"[121]

People came to him repeatedly to request that he should heal himself. He used to console them with the answer, "Everything will come right in due course." He also liked to explain to his devotees through metaphor why the continuation of the body meant nothing to him. Thus he used to say, "When a man goes to market with a basket and fills it with purchases and then carries it home on his head, does he not long to put down the load?" And, "When we have finished a meal do we keep the leaf-plate on which we have eaten it?" He also said, "You people talk of the tumour and name it Sarcoma Cancer. But believe me when I tell you that in my view there is no tumour, no Sarcoma Cancer at all."

On 1st May Dr. Raghavachari declared that amputation of the arm was unavoidable. But Ramana refused, "There is no need for alarm. The body is itself a disease. Let it have its natural end. Why mutilate it? Simple dressing of the affected part is enough."

This is the only instance when Ramana refused to accede to the wishes of the doctors. As a result the arm was not amputated.

The radium treatment finally had to be abandoned, as it was burning the skin and the wound frequently bled. As Ramana was becoming weaker, it was decided that a blood transfusion was necessary.

---

[120] S.S. Cohen's spiritual search brought him from Iraq to India. In 1936 he came to the Maharshi and built a hut at Palakothu.
[121] Cohen: Guru Ramana, p. 108

The doctors also thought that the sun would be beneficial for the sick arm. So they would arrange a seat for Ramana outside behind the cow shed, remove the bandage there and clean the wound. The affected part was then exposed to the sun's rays for some time. On one occasion devotees again expressed their worries and fears, but he merely joked about his bleeding ulcer, "See how nice it is! It is like a precious ruby. It has become an ornament to my arm. See how red it is! It is glowing brilliantly with the sun's rays falling on it. Look at it!"

The ayurvedic healer who had successfully treated Ramana's broken collarbone, tried a treatment using a poultice of healing green leaves. One evening Ramana returned from his walk shivering with fever and, walking with an extremely unsteady gait, was barely able to reach his couch. Shantamma, who could not control her grief at this sight, cried out, "Oh! Your body....", but before she was able to complete the sentence the Maharshi interrupted her, "Oho! The body? What about it? What has happened? Shivering? What if it is shivering? What you want is that there should be life in this body. Life is in it. Are you satisfied?" Finally he managed to control the shivering, and looking at the people around him, said, "This is *Nataraja's* dance. Daily it is a stationary *darshan*. Today it is tandava *darshan* [dancing *darshan*]. Why should there be any worry on that account?" Then he kept silent. The suspicion was that the shivering was caused by an infection brought on by the green leaves. So this treatment was stopped.

Sri Ramana found it increasingly difficult to climb the steps of the eastern entrance of the New Hall. When it was suggested that he should use the northern entrance, where the steps were not so high, he refused, as the northern part of the Hall was the women's area and he did not want to disturb them by entering there. But from now on, whenever he was not giving *darshan*, he remained in the small room on the eastern side of the New Hall, which had its own bath. This room became known as the 'Nirvana room', as it was here that he died.

Ramana continued with his daily routine for as long as possible. He would take his bath one hour before sunrise. Mornings and evenings he gave *darshan* at fixed times, he went through the Ashram post and supervised the printing of the Ashram publications. He was extremely attentive to everything and everybody, the only thing he paid no attention to was his illness. Nevertheless, more and more restrictions became necessary.

When one day the Ashram management decided that Sri Ramana needed more rest and kept the doors closed for several hours, he rebelled against their decision saying, "Many people come from great distances for *darshan* and cannot wait till evening; they must not be disappointed."

On 7th August the growth was removed for the third time by a well-organized team of doctors under the guidance of the renowned South Indian surgeon Dr. Guruswami Mudaliar. All the instruments he needed for the operation had been brought from a clinic in Madras. There were about thirty doctors present. As the electricity supply was unreliable, precautions were taken to avoid any power cuts during the operation.

Large numbers of devotees were also present and after the operation, when Ramana learned that so many people were waiting outside, he insisted on giving *darshan* for them on the veranda of the dispensary.

After the third operation the wound was again treated with radium and over the following months a slight improvement was noticed, so that once again people began to hope. But by the end of November the tumour had returned, this time higher up the arm. Day by day Ramana's strength was gradually ebbing away and his rheumatism was worsening. More than fifteen doctors came from Madras to decide if another operation was necessary; including Dr. Raghavachari. The District Medical Officer from Vellore also had a look at the growth. The doctors once again decided that another operation was needed.

Major Chadwick reports, "The night before this operation took place I went in to see Bhagavan and on my knees begged him not to have it. It was obvious it could do no good. Each time the tumour had grown bigger and bigger, spreading up his arm to the arm-pit. I prayed that this extra suffering was useless and that he would let us be spared the strain, but he refused, for, as he said, the doctors had taken so much trouble, it would be a shame to disappoint them now."[122]

The fourth operation was performed on 19th December. The doctors were in unanimous agreement that if the tumour were to return after this operation, then they would be unable to do anything more for him and the most they could do would be to relieve his pain. After the operation the Maharshi was very weak and hardly able to keep anything down. By now the wound had spread so that it covered nearly the whole of his upper arm.

T.S. Iyer, a homeopathic doctor famous throughout South India, was called in and started his treatment. The Maharshi's condition improved for a while and devotees again started to hope. The *darshan* hours could be prolonged to two hours each, mornings and evenings.

Sri Ramana moved definitively into the small Nirvana room. Each morning and evening he would sit on the veranda of the tiny room for one hour to give *darshan*. As the Nirvana room is very narrow, devotees were no longer able to sit in his presence as they did previously.

Various rumours circulated about the state of Ramana's health. A continuous stream of doctors visited the Ashram. Several renowned astrologers came to read his horoscope. It was said that the Maharshi did not have long to live, days perhaps, weeks at most.

---

[122] Sadhu Arunachala: Reminiscences, p. 78

Large crowds of people came for his 70th birthday (*jayanti*) celebrations on 5th January 1950. Sri Ramana stayed with them for several hours in the morning and evening.

The Final Attempts at Healing

In February another very painful growth appeared and grew rapidly in size. The tumour had now reached the shoulder and had spread inward. Again the doctors met to consult and this time decided there was no longer anything that could be done. Renowned ayurvedic doctors and homeopaths now tried their methods of treatment. The famous ayurvedic doctor Dr. Moos applied leeches, but in March he also gave up all hope. Other homeopaths tried their best with various diets, bandages and diathermic treatments, all to no avail. A blood test meanwhile revealed that Ramana was suffering from severe anaemia. In the opinion of the doctors the pains must have been unbearable, but he never complained. Although he sometimes remarked, "There is pain", he never said, "I am in pain". He used to make the anxious devotees laugh with his humorous remarks. His face retained its friendly smile and even became softer and kinder during the final months. Until the end his eyes glowed with their usual luminous power.

Roda McIver reports the following incident, "Worried about Bhagavan's health, in His last days, devotees would send Bhagavan all kinds of medicines and these were carefully arranged in a cupboard. One day He called for a big glass jar and ordered all the little bottles to be emptied into the jar and mixed well. He announced that He would take a spoonful every morning and evening. Some of the medicines were quite poisonous and we were scared. 'People send me these medicines out of their love for me. To please them I must take them all' argued Bhagavan! A doctor came and he too was terrified. The mixture was fantastic – allopathy, ayurvedic, homeopathy, herbs, biochemicals, ashes, powders, poisons – a lethal brew! Bhagavan was adamant. But when we invoked His own rule and demanded a spoonful for each of us, He relented and gave up the idea of drinking the stuff!"[123]

Meanwhile the Maharshi had become so famous in South India, that his sickness was reported in the press and on the radio. 'The Hindu', an English-language Madras newspaper, as well as the Tamil press and radio stations from Madras and Bombay reported on his condition. As a result more and more people flocked to the Ashram. It is reported that on 20th March there were around a thousand people at the Ashram from all parts of India and from abroad.

The treatment methods were also changed, in accordance with the devotees' instructions. Sri Ramana let them do so. But when he was asked by a devotee what should be tried next, he answered, "Have I ever asked for any treatment? It is you who want this and that for me, so it is you who must decide. If I were asked I should always say, as I have said from the beginning, that no treatment is necessary. Let things take their course."

All manner of treatments, both sensible and ridiculous, were tried, he was spared nothing. There were often violent disputes amongst the devotees about the right kind of treatment and a particular view would prevail for a while. When after some time its inefficacy became evident, it was abandoned and the next one was tried. In spite of all their efforts the Maharshi's condition continued to deteriorate. He felt constantly sick and could barely eat or pass water. In the end he could take only liquid food. The tumour had developed into a growth that looked like a cauliflower and was the size of a coconut.

On 19th March, the Telugu New Year, Sri Ramana had a bad accident. When he entered his bathroom in the morning, he stumbled over the threshold and fell. A devotee wanted to help him up, but he refused and stood up by himself, albeit with difficulty. His *koupina* and his towel were covered in blood. He probably had a

---

[123] Ganesan: Moments, p. 74

fracture, but his attendant was not allowed to make it public. The part of his body on which he had fallen, started to suppurate and was very painful, but this too was concealed. That day Ramana sat as usual from 9 a.m. onwards on the veranda of the little room to give *darshan*.

Soon afterwards his health deteriorated to such a point, that the *darshan* hours on the veranda could no longer be continued. He had to stay in the Nirvana room, while the devotees formed a queue and passed by the open door. As the numbers of visitors increased, those devotees who had until then been in close contact with him, could no longer speak with him. So they had no alternative but to join the long queue for a short silent glance.

The Final Days

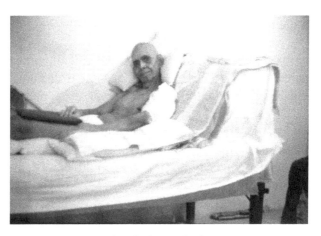

Ten days before mahanirvana

In the final days of his life in particular Sri Ramana consoled his devotees repeatedly with the same words, "They say I am dying, but I am not going away. Where could I go? I am here."

According to the report by S.S. Cohen on the 10th April there were so many devotees, that the *darshan* queues for both men and women had to be supervised by Ashram volunteers. "This *darshan* is no doubt a very great strain on the Maharshi, who, in his infinite compassion, keeps his face constantly turned towards the devotees the whole time the *darshan* lasts. His couch has east-west position and the door through which he looks at the devotees faces south, so that for one full hour he keeps his head turned in that direction and strains his neck. In his present state of health the strain on him must be great; yet he refuses to stop the *darshan*, or even reduce it to once a day.

His nourishment consisted today of a little fruit juice, tomato juice and some coconut water with glucose."[124]

On 11th April Sri Ramana's look at the evening *darshan* was especially intense. Some devotees felt so moved by this peculiar look of grace, that they interpreted it as his last. And they were proved right.

Narayana Iyer wrote to Professor Subbaramayya, "Bhagavan's condition was considered very critical. No liquid food even. No motions, no urine. Pulse very, very feeble. Blood-pressure very low. Heart weak. Temperature 96.8 and frequent hiccoughs ... Bhagavan asked in the evening if there was the queue in the morning. *Sarvadhikari* replied that it was suspended for sometime. Bhagavan said that He would suspend taking even a drop of water till all that came had their *darshan*. So there was the queue last evening. Bhagavan sat steady as before, suspending hiccoughs, pains and everything. After *darshan* I learnt that hiccough started. He is taking some food, that is, a little buttermilk and fruit juice. No medicines. His general condition is growing weaker."[125]

After this *darshan* the Maharshi no longer had enough strength to look at his devotees. S. S. Cohen reports on 12th April, "Today he is stretched full length on the sofa, with hollow eyes, sunken cheeks, pale, waxy skin and drained of vitality. Three attendants are

---

[124] Cohen: Guru Ramana, p. 140
[125] Subbaramayya: Reminiscences, p. 217

massaging hard his legs. The upper half of the body is exceedingly sensitive and cannot be touched without causing him severe pain. During the half-hour running *darshan* at 9 a.m. he could only at times turn his face to the devotees, but mostly he is listless. Doctors stopped testing and examining him and strictly forbade all access to his room."[126]

When on the morning of Thursday 13th April a doctor wanted to give him some medicine to relieve the congestion in his lungs, he told him that it would not be needed as within two days everything would come right.

14th April 1950

On the night before the 14th April Sri Ramana asked everyone to go to bed or to meditate and leave him alone. Even his attendants he sent away. The next morning he said in English to his attendant Rangaswami, who had just finished massaging him, "thanks". Rangaswami, who knew no English, looked astonished, so Sri Ramana smiled and explained the meaning to him, "The English have a word 'thanks', but we only say 'santosham' (I am pleased)."

In the morning and afternoon devotees passed by his open door in long queues. His tormented body was emaciated, his ribs were clearly visible and his skin had darkened, what people saw was a deeply distressing vision of suffering.

At midday when some liquid food was brought to him, he asked how late it was, but then added that henceforth time would no longer matter.

Until the last Sri Ramana showed his concern for the animals. Some hours before his death he asked if the peacocks, whom he heard screeching, had had their food. The animals reacted to his

---

[126] Cohen: Guru Ramana, p. 140

approaching end. The peacocks walked round his room, the cows, dogs, monkeys, birds, all showed their affection in their own way. But the white peacock stood on the roof of the Nirvana room screeching uninterruptedly.

After the evening *darshan* everyone realized that this had been the last one. The devotees stood in small groups outside, not leaving the small room, where the master lay, out of sight, and waited silently and in mourning for the end. Many eyes stared spellbound at the small window of the room in which he was dying. They could not see the Maharshi from here, but they could watch the movement of the two large fans, which were creating a slight breeze for him. As long as these fans continued to move, he was still alive. Inside the room there were about a dozen people, doctors and assistants. Ramana's body was supported by large cushions, so that he was almost sitting upright with his head leaning back and his mouth open. Two attendants were fanning him steadily to try and help him to breathe freely, as he had now started to struggle for breath. At 7 p.m. he was given oxygen for approximately 5 minutes, but as he felt that it brought no relief he asked for it to stop. Then he asked his attendants to sit him up straight. A group of *sadhus* and devotees who were sitting on the veranda of the Temple of the Mother opposite the small room, started to sing Akshara Mana Malai with the refrain 'Arunachala *Shiva*' and others joined in. When Sri Ramana heard the singing, he opened his bright, clear eyes, smiled briefly with an expression of indescribable goodness and tears of bliss rolled down his cheeks. At 8.47 p.m., without any struggle, his breathing stopped. There was no other sign of death, only that the next breath did not come.

At the exact minute of his death an object variously described as a shooting star or a meteor appeared on the horizon, moved slowly across the sky in the direction of Arunachala and disappeared behind its peak. The French photographer Henri Cartier-Bresson[127], who

---

[127] The famous photographer Henri Cartier-Bresson, who took the last pictures of Sri Ramana, also photographed the funeral of Gandhi. His photos can be seen in the copiously illustrated book 'In India'.

had been staying at the Ashram for two weeks, rushed into the Nirvana room shortly after the moment of the Maharshi's death and asked those present for the exact minute of his death. He later reported, "I was in the open space in front of my house, when my friends drew my attention to the sky, where I saw a vividly-luminous shooting star with a luminous tail, unlike any shooting star I had before seen, coming from the South, moving slowly across the sky and, reaching the top of Arunachala, disappeared behind it. Because of its singularity we all guessed its import and immediately looked at our watches – it was 8.47 – and then raced to the Ashram only to find that our premonition had been only too sadly true: the Master had passed into *mahanirvana* at that very minute."[128]

This unusual phenomenon was witnessed by large numbers of people over a wide area. On 16th April all English and Tamil newspapers published reports on the death of the Maharshi and also about the appearance of the shooting star.

The Funeral

Those devotees who had been waiting outside thronged towards the small room where the dead body lay. Many lost all self-control. The police immediately closed off the area. Later the corpse was placed in yoga posture in the middle of the big *darshan* hall, so that everyone was able to pay their last respects to the Maharshi. The news spread rapidly to the town and the surrounding villages, causing thousands of people to flock to the Ashram. S.S. Cohen reports about the following day, "The singing and chanting of Vedas continued throughout, as did the queue of worshippers till 11.30 a.m. today when the body was taken out to the South veranda for *puja* and *abhishikam*. Sri Niranjanananda Swami [Chinnaswami], the *Sarvadhikari*, assisted by his son Sri T. N. Venkataraman, poured over the sacred head dozens of pots of milk, curds, butter-milk, orange juice, mashed bananas and jackfruits, coconut water,

---

[128] Cohen: Guru Ramana, p. 144

etc., followed by many bottles of rose-water, attar, perfumes of all kinds and sweet smelling oils. Then enormous garlands of fresh roses and jasmines were placed round the neck and strewn all over the body."[129]

The place for the burial (*samadhi*) was dug out between the Old Hall and the northern wall of the Temple of the Mother. This spot had been agreed upon after a heated argument the previous night. The pit measured approximately 10 ½ feet by 10 ½ feet and was seven feet deep. The stonemasons isolated a small section in the middle with a wall. The rest was filled with several cartloads of sand from the sacred Ganges and the Narbada valleys.

At 6.30 p.m. the corpse was carried to the *samadhi* place in a decorated palanquin normally used for the temple goddess. It was placed in yoga posture in a bag made of the finest khaddar (homespun cotton cloth) which was then filled with pure camphor and lowered into the walled area. The pit was then filled to the edge with camphor, salt and sacred ashes to protect the sacred body from worms and rapid decomposition. Finally the pit was bricked up. The crowd of people was so large that the twenty policemen were barely able to keep them under control. Cohen reports that about 40,000 people came during the day to pay their last respects to Sri Ramana.

---

[129] dto., pp. 144ff

17. Sri Ramana´s Promise of His Continued Presence

They say I am dying, but I am not going away. Where could I go? I am here.

Before his death Sri Ramana repeated these words again and again. Of course his promise was meant in a wider sense and was not limited to his presence at the Ashram. But as the Maharshi spent 54 years of his life in Tiruvannamalai and 28 of them at Ramanashram, his presence is felt there with special intensity.

At first it did not seem that the Ashram could continue as a spiritual centre. After the death of the Maharshi people returned home or went on pilgrimage. Most of the devotees who had lived with Sri Ramana for a long time, packed their belongings and left. Balarama Reddy, for example, had already taken the decision to leave during the night of death, "When we came to know that Bhagavan had expired, Viswanatha Swami, Subbarao and I left the crowded, despairing scene at the Ashram and walked down the road, west of the Ashram. We sat on the bridge opposite the Draupadi Temple near the Dharmaraja Tank. Sitting there in a deeply reflective mood, we talked about Bhagavan and what we would all do, now that he was gone. With Bhagavan's physical absence, a new phase in our lives would begin. None of us thought we would stay in the Ashram, or even return to it once we left. ... Now it was all over (so we thought)."[130] And so, on the day after the funeral, he packed his belongings and left. Most of the devotees did the same.

Soon the Ashram was deserted. It is reported that thieves had even been able to break in in broad daylight. Financially Ramanashram was barely able to keep its head above water.

But gradually things changed. Devotees started to return. The understanding of what Sri Ramana had meant in his last promise, ripened in them. The overwhelming grief was gradually replaced by an overwhelming joy and the certitude of the continuing presence of the Master. Many devotees discovered a new kind of inner relationship to their *Sadguru*, feeling his presence more directly than ever.

The orderly daily routine, which was so characteristic of the Ashram, was kept after Sri Ramana's death. A management committee was formed, with Chinnaswami being chosen as its President. Shortly before his death in 1953 his son T.N. Venkataraman (Venkatoo) succeeded him and since 1994 the latter's eldest son, V.S. Ramanan has been the Ashram President.

At first a simple stone with a *lingam* was erected over Sri Ramana's burial spot, under a palm tree roof. Later an imposing *samadhi* was built, which was opened in 1967. Mornings and evenings the *Vedas* (*parayana*) are chanted, as was the custom during Ramana's lifetime. After the *parayana* a *puja* is celebrated at his burial spot.

---

[130] Reddy: Reminiscences, pp. 117ff

Samadhi Hall today

The favourite place for silent meditation from the very beginning was the Old Hall. In the small Nirvana room all the objects of Sri Ramana's daily use have been laid out:- his walking stick, the water jug, the peacock fan, the rotating bookshelf, his bed and much more.

Today Sri Ramanashram is a vibrant spiritual centre. More than 50 years after the death of the Maharshi it has lost nothing of its attraction, quite the opposite in fact. Ever more people, particularly in the West, have found in the person and teaching of Sri Ramana Maharshi their spiritual home and have chosen to make the pilgrimage to the place where he lived and taught for so long, so that their contact with him may gain in intensity.

It is, nevertheless, very important to point out that the true experience of the presence of Ramana and Arunachala must be in the Heart, it is not bound by time or place, and everything else has only the limited value of a manifestation. "Where could I go? I am here" means that he is the Heart of all living beings, the Self, as it states in Chapter X, verse 20 of the Bhagavad Gita, his favourite verse, "I am the Self, Oh Gudakesa, dwelling in the Heart of every being; I am the beginning, the middle and also the end of all living beings."

18. The Essential Features of the Teaching of Sri Ramana Maharshi

The Self, the Sole Reality,
Ever-existent, Formless Power
Taught of yore by the First of Teachers [Dakshinamurti],
As ever, through unbroken Silence –
The Primal Sound [akshara],
Who can reveal it in words?

This chapter is only an introduction to Sri Ramana´s teaching. For a deeper understanding it is recommended that the reader study the works written by and about him, such as the 'Collected Works', the 'Talks', 'Maharshi´s Gospel´, 'Be As You Are' and other collections of talks as given in the bibliography.

The Path of Self-Enquiry

Although Sri Ramana Maharshi was a spiritual master of the highest order, his teaching contains nothing which is new of itself. It belongs to the tradition of the Hindu *Advaita-Vedanta*, in which he found his own experience explained and interpreted. *Vedanta* means literally 'end of the *Vedas*' and is a school of philosophy in Hinduism which finds its profoundest expression in the *Upanishads*. *Vedanta* and *Advaita* are often used synonymously or in conjunction. One of the principal exponents of *Advaita-Vedanta* was *Shankara* who lived in the 8th century AD.

The fundamental teaching of *Advaita*, which literally means 'non-duality', is that the Absolute is not two, but only One. All manifestations are appearances within this one Reality. *Atman* (the divine within the human being) is identical with *Brahman* (the basis or source of the universe, the Absolute). Separate from this One Reality nothing exists: - there is no separate world, no separate God and no separate individual Ego. All is contained in *Brahman*. The feeling of being a separate, independent individual is the essential problem of the human condition. But how does this feeling of individuality arise at all?

Sri Ramana explains that individuality is nothing more than a thought or an idea. The I-thought 'I am' is the first thought which arises from the Heart-centre (for further details about the spiritual Heart see below), having arisen it identifies itself with the body, its actions and perceptions. (The term 'body' must be understood here in its fullest sense.) As a result, various thoughts and emotions arise which veil one's true identity. An individual subject sees itself as being separate from countless objects and an objective world. This individual 'I' now not only says about itself "I am", but further describes itself by saying "I am this or that" and "I am doing this and that."

Liberation according to Sri Ramana is found by reversing this process through Self-enquiry (Atma Vichara). One must, as it were, go back the way one came. He recommends asking oneself the question "Who am I?" The 'I' in this quest being the first I-thought, the I-feeling, on which all other thoughts and emotions are based. If one is able to keep one's attention on this pure I-consciousness, all other thoughts will be eliminated. Identification of the I-thought with the multitude of thoughts and objects will cease, as concentration on the I-thought severs this connection. In this way objects disappear as objects. Thoughts dissolve and finally even the first I-thought disappears. The true Self is revealed in its place. The mind sinks back into the spiritual Heart, whence it arose. The power of the Self draws it back to the place of its origin and finally totally destroys it, so that it can no longer arise. Only the Self remains. The ego is destroyed forever. This is what is known as 'Self Realization'. Henceforth everything is experienced as the one Self. The experience of the *jnani*, who has reached this final goal, is described as *sat-chit-ananda* (Being-Consciousness-Bliss).

Sri Ramana explains this search for the Self as follows, "You are the mind or think that you are the mind. The mind is nothing but thoughts. Now behind every particular thought there is a general thought which is the 'I', that is yourself. Let us call this 'I' the first thought. Stick to this I-thought and question it to find out what it is. When this question takes strong hold on you, you cannot think of other thoughts. ... What happens when you make a serious quest for the Self is that the I-thought as a thought disappears, something else from the depths takes hold of you and that is not the 'I' which commenced the quest. ... That is the real Self, the import of I. It is not the ego. It is the Supreme Being itself."[131]

And in his booklet 'Who am I?' (Nan Yar) it says that the enquiry at first may also be a mental process, but with continued practice it destroys all thoughts and at last itself. "By the inquiry 'Who am I?' the thought 'Who am I?' will destroy all other thoughts, and like the stick used for stirring the burning pyre, it will itself in the end get destroyed. Then, there will arise Self Realization."[132] In this way the I-thought - the feeling of being a separate personality – will be dissolved.

A visitor once asked, "How are these thoughts to be ended?" Ramana replied, "Find out their basis. All of them are strung on the single 'I'-thought. Quell it; all others are quashed." When the visitor asked further, "How to quell the 'I'-thought?" the answer was, "If its source is sought it does not arise, and thus it is quelled."[133]

And when being asked, "What is the means for constantly holding on to the thought 'Who am I?'", Sri Ramana explains in very precise terms, "When other thoughts arise, one should not pursue them, but should inquire: 'To whom did they arise? It does not matter how many thoughts arise. As each thought arises, one should inquire with diligence, 'To whom has this thought arisen?' The answer that would emerge would be, 'To me.' Thereupon if one inquires 'Who am I?' the mind will go back to its source; and the thought that arose will become quiescent. With repeated practice in this manner, the mind will develop the skill to stay in its source. When the mind that

---

[131] Sat-Darshana Bhashya, p. III
[132] Collected Works, p. 42
[133] Talks, p. 345 (from Talk 379)

is subtle goes out through the brain and the sense-organs, the gross names and forms appear; when it stays in the heart, the names and forms disappear. Not letting the mind go out but retaining it in the Heart is what is called 'inwardness' (antarmukha). Letting the mind go out of the Heart is known as 'externalization' (bahir-mukha). Thus, when the mind stays in the Heart, the 'I' which is the source of all thoughts will go, and the Self which ever exists will shine. Whatever one does, one should do without the egoity 'I'. If one acts in that way, all will appear as of the nature of *Shiva* (God)."[134]

The seeker has to practise this turning back continuously. Sri Ramana made no secret of the fact that it could be a lengthy struggle. When Sivaprakasam Pillai questioned him, "How long should inquiry be practised?" He answered, "As long as there are impressions of objects in the mind, the inquiry 'Who am I?' is required. As thoughts arise they should be destroyed then and there in the very place of their origin, through enquiry. If one resorted to contemplation of the Self unintermittently, until the Self was gained, that alone would do. As long as there are enemies within the fortress, they will continue to sally forth; if they are destroyed as they emerge, the fortress will fall into our hands."[135] And at another time he explained, "Abhyasa [practice] consists in withdrawal within the Self every time you are disturbed by thoughts. It is not concentration or destruction of the mind but withdrawal into the Self."[136]

But what remains when the ego is dissolved?

Sri Ramana, "People are afraid that when ego or mind is killed, the result may be a mere blank and not happiness. What really happens is that the thinker, the object of thought and thinking, all merge in the one Source, which is Consciousness and Bliss itself, and thus that state is neither inert nor blank. I don't understand why people should be afraid of that state in which all thoughts cease to exist and

---

[134] Collected Works. pp. 42ff (from 'Who am I')
[135] dto., p. 45
[136] Talks, p. 464 (from Talk 485)

the mind is killed. They are every day experiencing that state in sleep. There is no mind or thought in sleep. Yet when one rises from sleep one says, 'I slept happily'."[137]

The Maharshi stressed that the so called 'Self Realization' is neither a spectacular happening nor something new to be gained, "What is Self Realization? A mere phrase. People expect some miracle to happen, something to drop from Heaven in a flash. It is nothing of the sort. Only the notion that you are the body, that you are this or that, will go, and you remain as you are. Indeed, Realization is but another name for the Self."[138] And elsewhere he says, "It is false to speak of Realization. What is there to realize? The real is as it is, ever. How to real-ize it? All that is required is this. We have real-ized the unreal, i.e. regarded as real what is unreal. We have to give up this attitude. That is all that is required for us to attain *jnana*."[139]

He also describes Realization of the Self as follows, "In a pinhole camera, when the hole is small, you see shapes and colours. When the hole is made big, the images disappear and one sees only clear light. Similarly when the mind is small and narrow, it is full of shapes and words. When it broadens, it sees pure light. When the box is destroyed altogether, only the light remains."[140]

Although Sri Ramana supported all spiritual paths, he untiringly and expressly recommended Self-enquiry as the most effective path, in which all other paths finally merge. He constantly advised seekers to ask themselves the question, "Who am I?" When a confessed atheist provocatively asked him, "Is there God; can you prove the existence of God." he smiled and replied, "Why worry about God? Let Him worry about Himself! Find out who raises the question." The atheist was puzzled. Sri Ramana recommended that he read the book 'Who am I?' The visitor, who only wanted to stay for a few hours, ended up staying for several days. Finally he said, "Bhagavan! When I

---

[137] Mudaliar: Day by Day, p. 65
[138] Subbaramayya: Reminiscences, p. 138
[139] Mudaliar: Day by Day, p. 88
[140] Tales of Bhagavan. In Ramana Smrti, p. [95]

came here as an atheist, denying God, I was happy. But, now, after asking myself the question 'Who am I?' I am thoroughly confused. I feel I have deteriorated; therefore I am very unhappy." Sri Ramana smiled at him and said, "Your confusion is not a state of deterioration. All these days you have been indifferent to the truth behind your own existence. Now you have raised the fundamental question; thereby you have moved away from indifference. So it is only an improvement! From indifference to confusion, from confusion to clarity, from (intellectual) clarity to experience and from experience to abidance in the Self – this is the order of ascendancy in spiritual *sadhana*."[141]

The Spiritual Heart

Sri Ramana liked to speak about the 'Heart' (hridayam) as the place of the spiritual experience. The 'Heart' referred to is not the physical heart, but the spiritual Heart, which is on the right side, two finger-widths to the right of the middle of the chest. There dwells the experience of one's true identity. This can be demonstrated in everyday experience by the fact that people intuitively point to this spot when pointing to themselves. The I-thought arises here. "Hridayam=hrit+ayam = this is the centre. It is that from which thoughts arise, on which they subsist and where they are resolved. The thoughts are the content of the mind and, they shape the universe. The Heart is the centre of all."[142]

The teaching about the spiritual Heart did not originate with Sri Ramana himself. He found it and adopted it, as it corresponded to his own experience. In the Maha Narayana *Upanishad* which is one of the sacred Hindu scriptures it says, "It must be understood that the Heart resembling the lotus, a span below the throat and a span above the navel hangs upside down and is the chief seat of the Universal form of *paramatman*."[143]

---

[141] Purushottama Ramana, p. [10
[142] Talks, p. 92 (from Talk 97)
[143] transl. in: Sadhu Arunachala: Reminiscences, p. 97

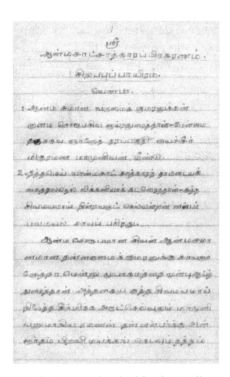

Sri Ramana's handwriting in Tamil

Sri Ramana's teaching about the Heart is found in particular in the famous verse included in Ganapati Muni's 'Ramana Gita' and which has already been quoted in chapter 8,

"In the interior of the Heart-cave *Brahman* alone shines in the form of the *atman* with direct immediacy as I, as I. Enter into the Heart with questing mind or by diving deep within or through control of breath, and abide in the *atman*."

The Sanskrit verse starts with "Hridaya kuhara madhye", "in the interior of the Heart-cave". The sacred Hindu scriptures stress that *Brahman* shines in the heart of all living beings. Sri Ramana takes up this statement and develops it in more detail. In the cave of the Heart, i.e. in its inmost centre, *atman*, which is identical with *Brahman* is experienced as 'I-I'. 'I-I' means continuous Self-consciousness, Self-awareness, which is in each person's immediate experience, and which cannot be doubted, even in deep-sleep. 'I-I' is the true 'I' or Self, which was already there, is eternal and never changing. The individual I, the changeable and unsteady ego, has its source here. If the I-thought is traced back to its origin and merges there, it finally comes to an end there forever, and this is 'Self Realization'.

In this verse three paths are mentioned by which one can enter the Heart: - the path of Self-enquiry, the path of diving deep and the path of breath control. Sri Ramana's teaching concentrates mainly on Self-enquiry. "Diving deep" is explained by the example of the pearl-diver, which Ramana gives in 'Nan Yar' saying that just as the pearl-diver ties a stone round his waist, holds his breath and concentrates one-pointedly on his single goal, which is to dive into the sea in order to find the precious pearl, likewise the seeker should dive into the Heart.

The path of breath-control does not refer to pranayama as practised in hatha yoga, but simply to watching the breath, as is practised in some forms of Zen meditation, as mind and breath have the same root, as Ramana repeatedly stressed. If the breath is watched, it comes to rest.

Whatever means one uses, the important thing is the goal, which is to reach the Heart and remain there forever, to be it. In the Heart, Self-enquiry finds its end, it dissolves in the realisation of the Heart, as Sri Ramana once said, "What is finally realized as a result of such enquiry into the Source of Aham-vritti [I-thought] is verily the Heart as the undifferentiated Light of pure Consciousness, into which the reflected light of the mind is completely absorbed."[144]

In its deepest meaning the spiritual Heart is identical with the Self (*atman*), God and Guru and in the final analysis not restricted to any particular spot in the body. To a question from a disciple about the meaning of the Heart Sri Ramana answered, "Call it by any name,

---

[144] Maharshi's Gospel, p. 83. About the spiritual Heart see also in the same book part II, chapters 4 and 5.

God, Self, the Heart or the Seat of Consciousness, it is all the same. The point to be grasped is this, that Heart means the very Core of one's being, the Centre, without which there is nothing whatever."[145] And elsewhere, "The Heart is not physical. Meditation should not be on the right or the left. Meditation should be on the Self. Everyone knows 'I am'. Who is the 'I'? It will be neither within nor without, neither on the right nor on the left. 'I am' – that is all."[146]

Teaching through Silence

Sri Ramana was and is, first and foremost, a master who teaches through silence. His deepest teaching is found neither in his spoken answers to seekers, nor in his written works, but in his powerful silence – because the Truth transcends all words. His method of teaching is often compared to that of *Dakshinamurti,* who is the young *Shiva,* seated under a banyan tree. At his feet are his four disciples, whom he taught through silence only. He is seen as the guru of all gurus and represents the ascetic aspect of *Shiva.* His statue can be found in every temple in Southern Indian.

One evening, devotees asked Sri Ramana to explain the meaning of *Shankara's* hymn in praise of *Dakshinamurti* (*Dakshinamurti Stotram*). They waited for his answer, but in vain. The Maharshi sat motionless on his seat, in total silence.

The intense power and peace of his presence enveloped all those present to such a degree that they sat through the night, without any of them noticing the passage of time. In this way eight hours passed by. When finally Ramana stood up to go for his morning walk, the others became aware for the first time that it was now morning. For the whole night he had been commenting upon the meaning of *Shankara's* verses by his example. The next day he said to his devotees, "True Silence means abiding in the Self."

---

[145] dto., p.66
[146] Talks, p. 229 (from Talk 273)

The silent teacher

On another occasion he explained, *"Dakshinamurti*, i.e., the great *Shiva* himself could not express the truth of the one Reality except by silence. But that silence could not be understood except by the very advanced. The others have to be told."[147]

How powerful Sri Ramana's silence was, is illustrated by the following episode, which the cook Shantamma has recorded for us, "One morning a European came in a horse carriage to the Ashram and went straight to Bhagavan. He wrote something on a piece of paper and showed it to Bhagavan. Bhagavan did not answer; instead he gazed at the stranger with unwinking eyes. The stranger was staring back at him. Then Bhagavan closed his eyes and the stranger also closed his. They stayed without moving. At mealtime the meals were served but Bhagavan would not open his eyes. Madhavaswami, the attendant, got Bhagavan's water pot and stood ready to lead Bhagavan out of the Hall. Bhagavan would not stir. We felt afraid to go near, such was the intensity around him. His face was glowing with a strange light. The guests in the dining hall were waiting and the food before them was getting cold. Chinnaswami was talking

---

[147] Mudaliar: Day by Day, p. 22

loudly to attract Bhagavan's attention. Even vessels were banged about, but all in vain. When the clock was striking twelve Bhagavan opened his eyes. They were glowing very brightly. Madhavaswami took up the water jug; the European got into the carriage and went away. It was the last we saw of him. We did not even get his name."[148]

---

[148] Shantamma: Eternal Bhagavan. In: Ramana Smrti, p. [83]

Chronological Table

30.12.1879	Birth of Venkataraman in Tiruchuli
1892	Death of his father Sundaram Iyer and move to Madurai to live with his uncle Subba Iyer
Nov. 1895	Ramana hears from a relative about the holy hill Arunachala
July 1896	Death experience, which leads him to Self Realization
29.8.1896	Spontaneous departure to Arunachala
1.9.1896	Arrival at Tiruvannamalai; residence in various parts of the Arunachaleswara temple
From Feb. 1897	In Gurumurtam and in the mango grove
May 1898	Ramana's whereabouts discovered; his uncle Nelliappa Iyer visits him in order to bring him back home
From Sept. 1898	Lives for several months in Pavalakkunru
Dec. 1898	Unsuccessful attempt by his mother Alagammal and his elder brother Nagaswami to bring him back home
1899 -1916	In Virupaksha Cave and Mango Tree Cave
1900 -1902	Ramana gives written answers to questions from his first disciples (Vichara Sangraham and Nan Yar)
18.11.1907	Ganapati Muni's first meeting with Ramana
1912	Second death experience at Tortoise Rock
1913 -1914	Two visits by mother; Akshara Mana Malai and other hymns in praise of Arunachala
1916	Alagammal takes up permanent residence with her son in the Virupaksha Cave
1916 -1922	In Skandashram
1918	Ramana's younger brother Nagasundaram joins the Ashram community
19.5.1922	Death and liberation of the mother

Dec. 1922	Ramana takes up residence near his mother's grave; Ramanashram comes into being
1923 -1929	Upadesa Saram, Upadesa Manjari and Ulladu Narpadu (with supplementary verses)
1930s and 40s	Translations of important *Advaita* scriptures into Tamil, Malayam and Telugu; Arunachala Pancharatna in Sanskrit
Feb. 1949	Ramana taken ill with cancer
14.4.1950	Death of the Maharshi; a glorious shining star seen to move in the direction of Arunachala
15.4.1950	Funeral of Ramana Maharshi

Glossary

abhishekam: ceremonial bathing of a statue or sacred image

adina guru: founder of a *math* and/or line or succession of gurus

advaita: non-duality, i.e. the absolute is not two; the fundamental teaching of *Vedanta*; a philosophical school

agamas: source of the teaching, holy scriptures, traditional texts

annas: 16 annas are 1 rupee; today the coin is no longer in circulation

Arudra Darshan: (lit. 'the sight of *Shiva'*). On this day the victory of *Shiva Nataraja* over the demon Andhaka (the dark, the blind) is celebrated. When *Shiva* defeated the demon, he danced his cosmic dance which is an expression of highest joy and keeps the whole universe alive.

Ashtavakra Gita: a Sanskrit work on *Advaita-Vedanta* from the time of the younger *Upanishads*. It is a dialogue between Ashtavakra and his disciple Janaka in which they discuss the highest flights of *advaita.*

Atma Bodha: one of the works of *Shankara*

atman: the Self, the inner principle of the human being; originally: life-breath

betel: hard, dark red nut, whose juice aids digestion

Bhagavad Gita: the song of God; spiritual teaching poetry with 700 verses; the teaching of Sri Krishna

Bhagavan: God; also used when referring to a Saint, who is seen to be One with God (or Self); it expresses the special veneration of the disciple towards his master. Sri Ramana neither suggested that people should address him like this, nor contradicted them when they did.

bhakti: love, devotion; with particular reference to spiritual love and devotion to God, Self and/or Guru

bhiksha: alms received through begging

Brahma: the one impersonal universal spirit (*Brahman*) manifested as a personal Creator; the Creator, seen as part of the Trinity, together with *Vishnu*, the preserver, and *Shiva*, the destroyer. Worship of Brahma, as the Creator, is not as popular as the worship of *Shiva* and *Vishnu*.

Brahmachari: (celibate) student; the first of four stages of life according to the vedic view

Brahman: the route >brh< means, lit. growth, expansion, evolution, strength, intensity; the absolute; the source of all being, the essence in all things, the absolute unmanifest. Brahman and *atman* are one according to the teaching of the *Upanishads*, *Vedanta* and also according to Ramana Maharshi. The absolute is *sat-chit-ananda* (being–awareness–bliss).

Brahmin: member of the upper caste, originally of the priest caste

brinjal: aubergine

cella: the sanctum sanctorum in a temple

chakra meru: pyramid-shaped energy diagram, which symbolises the godly order of the cosmos. It often is worshipped as a sacred design. Sri Chakra is the universe expressed and resolved in a circular diagram (yantra) which can be used for deep contemplation. Mount Meru is, symbolically, the axis at the centre of the body (microcosm) and at the centre of the universe (macrocosm).

Dakshinamurti: the south-facing god; *Shiva* as the young god, who teaches through silence

Dakshinamurti Stotram: a hymn by *Shankara* in honour of Dakshinamurti

darshan: vision; the formal visit of a pupil to his guru; sight, especially the graceful glance, which the master gives his pupil

dhal: dish made of different kinds of lentils

dharma: essential characteristics; true nature

dhoti: long strip of cloth, which is worn by men like a skirt

dosas: pancakes made with flour of rice or lentils; popular in the Southern Indian breakfast

Ellam Ondre: *Vedanta* text from the 19th century

Ganesha: god with an elephant head, son of *Shiva* and Parvati

giri: mountain, hill

giri-pradakshina: circuit of the hill

gopuram: temple tower, especially in Southern Indian temple compounds

gurukkal: priest in a *Shiva*-temple

iddlies: round, steamed cakes made with the flour of rice and chickpeas

Isvara: god as the Highest Lord and Creator of the universe; usual form of address for *Shiva*; also the personal god

japa: whisper, muttered prayer; the incessant, focussed repetition of a name of god or a *mantra*, with the aim of silencing and steadying the mind

jayanti: birthday

jnana: knowledge; cognition

jnana-yoga: path to realization through knowledge; the immediate realization of the *advaita* teaching *jnana:* one who has reached the goal of *jnana-yoga*, which is realization through knowledge

Kaivalya Navaneeta: famous Tamil scripture, circa 15th century

kamandala: water vessel used by ascetics

karma: action; result of action; the results of the good or bad actions carried on in this or another life; law of balanced justice; cause and effect

Kartikai: Tamil month in November/December

Kartikai Deepam: light festival on Arunachala, in which *Shiva* manifests himself as a *lingam* of fire

koupina: a kind of loincloth; a strip of cloth which just covers the abdomen

kumbhabhiseka: sanctification; opening of a temple

lingam: mark, sign, symbol for *Shiva*: a stone in form of a cylinder which is rounded on top

mahanirvana: great (or final) liberation; here: death of a great human being

mahapuja: maha = big; the big *puja*; feast on occasion of the day of death of Sri Ramana's mother

Maharshi: maha = great, rishi = seer, singer, sage; great rishi, especially those saints of early time, who had the vision of the vedic revelation. This title was given to Sri Ramana by Ganapati Muni.

maha-yoga: great yoga

mantapam: hall, especially a columned hall in or near a temple

mantra: a short formula from the holy scriptures, a word or only a syllable. The mantra is repeated (see *japa*). The ultimate mantra is the syllable 'om'.

math: institution of spiritual education in remembrance of a saint. In the bigger maths, *sadhus* live in groups, similar to a monastery.

mauna: silence; the condition of the Sage (*muni*)

mauni: one who has taken a vow of silence

maya: illusion; the power of *Brahman* which appears as the manifest condition of the world

Meenakshi: The king's daughter Meenakshi (the fish-eyed) is an incarnation of *Shiva's* consort Parvati.

moksha: liberation, redemption from the circle of birth, death and reincarnation

mukti: identical with *moksha*

muni: sage, ascetic

Nataraja: natya = dance; king of the dancers; *Shiva's* cosmic dance symbolises creation, preservation and destruction, but likewise rebirth, life and liberation

paramatman: the highest *atman* (the highest Self), which is identical with *Brahman*

parayana: singing of the *Vedas* or other religious texts

payasam: sweet thick paste of grain, milk, sugar and sometimes with fruits

Periyapuranam: collection of legends about saints from the 12th century AD; it is the second volume of the Tamil-Veda (Tirumurai), a canonical collection of Tamil religious literature. The 63 Nayanars (saints) shaped the *bhakti*-period, which started around 600 AD in India and which heralded a new spiritual awakening of devotion to God *Shiva*, finding expression in simple poetical language. The famous trinity amongst them are the saints Appar, Sundarar and Sambandar, who visited many of the Southern India temples and shrines and composed many songs which epitomise the highest flights of devotion in their praise.

pradakshina: pra = forwards, dakshina = southern, in southern direction; clockwise circuit of an object of devotion. The origin of pradakshina is rooted in the observation of astronomical events and represents a simple imitation of the course of the sun. Therefore the circuit always starts in the east and is carried out clockwise, with the venerated object always on the right-hand side. The sun is the symbol of life. Contra-rotation is the symbol of death. Therefore in the cult of the dead the funeral pyre of the deceased is rounded by the eldest son in an anti-clockwise direction.

prarabdha (karma): that part of *karma* which must be worked out in this life

prasad: grace; gift or consecrated food, which has been offered to a saint, guru or God and then given back to the believer or distributed among the devotees; a gift from a saint

puja: ceremonial worship with flowers, water etc.

Puranas: a class of holy texts from the 6th to 16th century AD, which contains extensive collections of legends about the trinity of gods *Brahma*, *Vishnu* and *Shiva*

puris: unleavened bread made from wheat

raja-yoga: system of yoga, as taught by Patanjali

rasam: very spicy soup

Ribhu Gita: advaitic Sanskrit-text of round 2000 verses

rishi: seer, enlightened, interpreter of the vedic hymns; see also *Maharshi*

sadguru: fully enlightened guru; the true Guru

sadhana: methodical spiritual practice

sadhu: one who is dedicated to God; a wandering monk or ascetic; a spiritual seeker, who renounces profession and family; often used as a synonym of *sannyasin*

sahaja: natural

sahaja samadhi: the natural state of effortless, permanent Self Realization, in which the ego-mind has dissolved completely. For the realized, *sahaja* is the natural state.

samadhi: absorption in the Self, highest state of meditation; also used when referring to bodily death and/or a place of burial

sambar: very spicy sauce taken with rice in South Indian meals

samsara: circle of birth and death

sannyasa: renunciation, fourth stage of life for a Brahmin

sannyasin: wandering monk, someone who has taken a vow of *sannyasa* and dedicates his life to striving to attain enlightenment and therefore gives up family and profession; as an outer sign s/he often wears the ochre robe. *Shankara*, the reviver/codifier of *Advaita-Vedanta* in the 8th century AD founded the four main *sannyas*-orders/*maths*, in the south, north, east and west.

sarvadhikari: leader of an institution; here: Ashram-manager

sastri: scholar of holy scriptures and traditions

sat: pure Being; Truth; Reality

sat-chit-ananda: a description of *Brahman* and *atman* as 'Being (*sat*), Consciousness (chit) and Bliss (ananda)

satsang: association with Being; association with the wise or inner contact with the Self

shakti: power of *Shiva*, the godly power, through which creation comes into being; the consort of *Shiva*, the Mother Goddess, who is worshipped throughout India under various names

Shankara: 788-820; main representative of *Advaita-Vedanta* and reviver of Hinduism

shastras: holy scriptures of Hinduism; the *Vedas* and other scriptures, statute books and commentaries

Shiva: Shiva is the double-faced God, who embodies the aspect of dissolving and destruction and likewise as the beneficent lets all come into being. He symbolises absolute Being and is the destroyer of ignorance and ego.

shruti: hearing, listening; the holy scriptures of the Hindus

siddhi: supernatural power; accomplishment, attainment

Skanda: lit. jumper or hopper; name of the god of war and the son of *Shiva* and Parvati

Sri: saint, blessed; today also used as a general address of respect like 'Sir'

Subrahmanya: younger son of *Shiva* and Parvati, Ganesha's brother

Swami: owner, lord, master; a form of address for the spiritual teacher; occasionally it is also used as a form of respect (e.g. Mr.); (also an epithet of *Skanda*)

tapas: heat, fire; austerity, ascetic exercise

teertham: holy place of bathing; often it is a square pond with steps leading down to the water

Tevaram: consists of the first 7 books of the 12 volume Tamil-Veda (Tirumurai) and contains the collection of hymns of the three great Tamil poets and saints Sambandar, Appar and Sundarar from the 7th and 8th century AD

Thayumanavar: saint of the 18th century, whose religious poems have become very popular

Tiruvasagam: 8th book of the Tamil-*Veda*

upadesa: teaching, instruction

Upanishads: secret teaching, these texts are the basis of *Vedanta*. The oldest *Upanishads* perhaps codified circa 800-700 BCE.

uppuma: thick wheat-paste with fried vegetables and spices

vasanas: habits of the mind, mindstuff; latent tendencies in the mind which originate out of former thoughts, desires and actions

Veda: knowledge, revelation

Vedas: the earliest scriptures of Hinduism

Vedanta: the end and likewise fulfilment of the *Vedas*; the teaching of the *Upanishads*

vibhuti: sacred ash; manifestation of *Shiva's* eightfold power

Vishnu: preserver, protector and sustainer of the universe; one of the Trinity

Vivekachudamani: a well known scripture, credited to *Shankara*, which examines the path of discrimination and enquiry

Yoga Vasistha: one of the major works on *advaita* (6th-11th century)

Bibliography

Bhagavan Sri Ramana: A Pictorial Biography. – 2nd ed. –Tiruvannamalai, 1985

Bhatt, G.P.: The Skanda-Purana. – 1st ed. - Delhi, 1992 – (Ancient Indian Tradition and Mythology Series, Vol. 49-63) (Vol. 51 contains Arunachala Puranam)

Brunton, Paul: Conscious Immortality. – 2nd ed. – Tiruvannamalai, 1998

Cohen, S.S.: Guru Ramana: Memories and Notes. – 6th ed. – Tiruvannamalai, 1993

The Collected Works of Ramana Maharshi. – 6th rev. ed. – Tiruvannamalai, 1996

Ganesan, V.: Moments Remembered: Reminiscences of Bhagavan Ramana. – 2nd ed. – Tiruvannamalai, 1994

Ganesan, V.: Purushottama Ramana: – 4. ed. – Bangalore, 1997

Godman, David: Be As You Are: The Teachings of Sri Ramana Maharshi. – Tiruvannamalai, 1985

Godman, David: The Power of the Presence: Part One. – Tiruvannamalai, 2000

Godman, David: The Power of the Presence: Part Two. – Tiruvannamalai, 2001

Godman, David: The Power of the Presence: Part Three. – Tiruvannamalai, 2002

The Guru and the Disciple: Bhagavan Ramana and Ganapati Muni. – Bangalore, 1998

Humphreys, Frank H.: Glimpses of the Life and Teachings of Bhagavan Sri Ramana Maharshi. – 3rd reprint. – Tiruvannamalai, 1996

The Inner Circle. – ed. and comp. by A.R. Natarajan. – 2nd ed. - Bangalore, 1996

Iyer, T.K. Sundaresa: At the Feet of Bhagavan. – 1st ed. – Tiruvannamalai, 1980

Krishna, G.: Nayana. – Madras, 1978

Kunjuswami: Reminiscences. – Tiruvannamalai, 1992

The Last Days and Maha-Nirvana of Bhagavan Sri Ramana. – Tiruvannamalai, 1991

Mahadevan, T.M.P.: Ramana Maharshi: The Sage of Arunachala. – London, 1977

Mahadevan, T.M.P.: Ramana Maharshi and His Philosophy of Existence. – 2nd ed. – Tiruvannamalai, 1967

The Maharshi Newsletter. – New York (journal of Arunachala Ashrama, NY)

Maharshi's Gospel: The Teachings of Sri Ramana Maharshi. - 11th ed. – Tiruvannamalai, 1994

Mouni Sadhu: In Days of Great Peace. – 2nd ed. – London, 1957

The Mountain Path. – Tiruvannamalai, 1964 ff (journal of Ramanashram)

Mudaliar, A. Devaraja: Day by Day with Bhagavan. – 3rd reprint. – Tiruvannamalai, 1989

Mudaliar, A. Devaraja: My Recollections of Bhagavan Sri Ramana. – rev. ed. - Tiruvannamalai, 1992

Muruganar: The Garland of Guru's Sayings. – Tiruvannamalai, 1996

Muruganar: Homage to the Presence of Sri Ramana. - Tiruvannamalai, 1994

Nagamma, Suri: Letters from and Recollections of Sri Ramanasramam. – 2nd ed. - Tiruvannamalai, 1992

Nagamma, Suri: Letters from Sri Ramanasramam Volumes I & II. – 3rd ed. – Tiruvannamalai, 1985

Nagamma, Suri: My Life at Sri Ramanasramam. – 2nd ed. – Tiruvannamalai, 1993

Nambiar, K.K.: The Guiding Presence of Sri Ramana. – 1st ed. – Tiruvannamalai, 1984

Narasimha Swami: Self Realization: The Life and Teachings of Sri Ramana Maharshi. – Tiruvannamalai, 1997

Natarajan, A.R.: Bhagavan Ramana and Mother. – Bangalore, 3rd ed., 1997

Natarajan, A.R.: Timeless in Time: Sri Ramana Maharshi. – Bangalore, 1999

Osborne, Arthur: The Collected Works of Ramana Maharshi. – York Beach, 1997

Osborne, Arthur: Ramana-Arunachala. – 6th ed. – Tiruvannamalai, 1994

Osborne, Arthur: Ramana Maharshi and the Path of Self-Knowledge. – York Beach, 1995

Osborne, Arthur: The Teachings of Ramana Maharshi. – 1st ed. – York Beach, 1996

Ramana, Shankara and the Forty Verses: The Essential Teachings of Advaita. – London, 2002

Ramana Smrti. – 1st ed. – Tiruvannamalai, 1980

Reddy, N. Balarama: My Reminiscences. – 1st ed. – Tiruvannamalai, 1996

Sadhu Arunachala: A Sadhu´s Reminiscences of Ramana Maharshi. – 5th ed. – Tiruvannamalai, 1994

Sadhu Om: The Path of Sri Ramana: Part I. – 5th ed. – Tiruvannamalai, 1997

Sadhu Om: The Path of Sri Ramana: Part II. – Sec. print. - Tiruvannamalai, 1997

Shankaranarayanan, S.: Bhagavan and Nayana. – 1st ed. – Tiruvannamalai, 1983

Spiritual Stories as told by Ramana Maharshi. – 3rd ed. – Tiruvannamalai, 1992

Sri Ramana Gita. – 8th ed. - Tiruvannamalai, 1998

Subbaramayya, G.V.: Sri Ramana Reminiscences. – 3rd ed. – Tiruvannamalai, 1994

Swarnagiri, Ramananda: Crumbs from His Table. – 5th ed. – Tiruvannamalai, 1981

Taleyarkhan, Feroza: Sages, Saints and Arunachala Ramana. – Madras, 1970

Talks with Sri Ramana Maharshi. – 9th ed. – Tiruvannamalai, 1994

Unforgettable Years: Memoirs of 29 old devotees of Bhagavan Sri Ramana Maharshi. – 3rd ed. – Bangalore, 1997

The Vedaparayana at Sri Ramanasramam. – 2nd ed. – Tiruvannamalai, 1985

CPSIA information can be obtained
at www.ICGtesting.com
Printed in the USA
BVHW041414080620
581024BV00005B/223

9 783739 210391